PRACTICE BOOK

COAST TO COAST

Harcourt Brace & Company

Orlando Atlanta Austin Boston San Francisco Chicago Dallas New York Toronto London

CONTENTS

Printed in the United States of America

ISBN 0-15-307418-3

9 10 11 12 13   054   03 02 01 00

You will need

a notebook or stapled sheets of paper, a pencil, a pen, crayons or markers.

MAKING A LEARNING LOG

Here are some ideas for making and using your Learning Log:

★ Illustrate the cover with drawings that will help make this book a fun place to write.

★ You may want to divide your book into sections. For example, you could keep a section for each subject, or you might divide the book into weeks or months.

★ Keep your Learning Log with you as much as possible. You never know when you'll learn something new.

★ Try to write in your Learning Log at least once each day.

I have sections for Reading, Language, Math, Science, and Social Studies in mine.

I drew a picture of a space shuttle on mine. That reminds me of how much there is to learn.

You can record all kinds of things in your Learning Log:

★ You might **tell _how_** you learned something. -------->

> November 11
> I learned a great way to summarize. I wrote a one-sentence summary for each section of the article. I highlighted the important words. Then I wrote a new sentence using the highlighted words.

★ You could **write what you know** and **what you don't know** about a topic. -------->

> I know that whales are mammals, but I really want to find out whether they have lungs, as most mammals do.

★ You might **write questions** or **list things** you want to learn better. -------->

> THINGS TO STUDY
> 1. USING <u>LESS</u> OR <u>FEWER</u>
> 2. USING <u>WHO</u> OR <u>WHOM</u>
> 3. USING <u>WHICH</u> OR <u>THAT</u>

★ You can **make diagrams** or **charts**. -------->

> helps strangers   is kind to animals
>
> (main character)
>
> works hard   is honest

★ You could **write about** how what you learned could be applied to **other subjects** or your **daily life**. -------->

> Using context clues will help me in science. I always seem to run into lots of unfamiliar words in the science textbook.

Look for the TRY THIS! Learning Log activities throughout this book. They'll give you ideas about other things to write in your Learning Log.

Name _____

Read the boldfaced words and their definitions in the box below. Then, on each line in the letter that follows, write the word from the box that best completes the sentence.

demonstration:	a public showing of how something works
muffle:	to deaden or soften a sound
partition:	something that divides, as a wall or a screen
prowls:	roams about secretly and quietly
prose:	any writing or speech that is not poetry

Dear Dad,

Do you remember the _____ you put up in my room last month? It was supposed to separate my study area from any distractions, such as TV. Well, we have a slight problem now. The dog doesn't like it because there's no room for her near my desk. She just _____ around my room while I'm studying. Every now and then she barks to show her frustration. There is no way to _____ the sound, of course, so I'm thinking of removing the temporary wall. Maybe the dog will keep quiet if she can sit by me while I work.

I'm working on an interesting assignment for school now. We have to choose a passage of _____ and write some poetry based on it. I'm trying to imitate the writing style of other poetry I have read. When you get back from your trip, I'll give you a _____ by reading the poetry aloud. OK? See you soon.

Love,

Leigh

List three vocabulary words on a separate sheet of paper. For each word, write another word that could be used to describe it.

Name _____

A. Summarize "Dear Mr. Henshaw" by completing the story map.

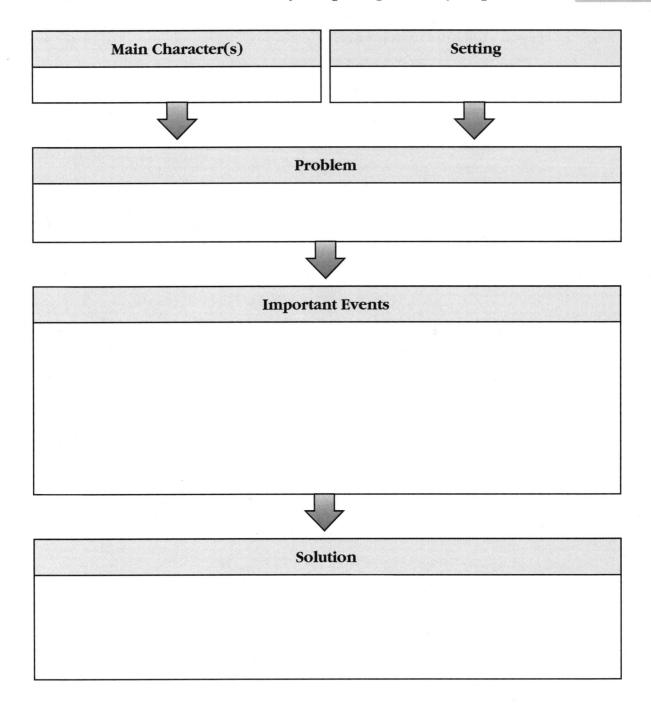

Main Character(s)	Setting

Problem

Important Events

Solution

B. Tell how Leigh Botts changes by the ending of the story.

_____

_____

_____

Name _____

A. When author Janet Yee visited Mr. Dawson's fifth-grade class, everyone had something to say. This script records part of the discussion, but all the end punctuation marks are missing. Add a period, a question mark, or an exclamation point at the end of each sentence.

Miko: I just finished reading your new book, Ms. Yee
It's fabulous

Ms. Yee: Well, I'm glad you liked it Which part was
your favorite

Miko: There were lots of great parts, but my favorite
was the chase scene

Jasmine: Oh, did you really like that part best I thought
the part about the raft trip was much better

Tomas: I think you both chose good sections, but not
the very best I liked the descriptions, especially
the descriptions of their meals Do you remember
that supper cooked over the campfire

Mr. Dawson: I remember that scene It made me hungry
Who else has a favorite scene from Ms. Yee's book

B. Write three sentences that these other students might contribute to the discussion. Make one of your sentences declarative, one interrogative, and one exclamatory. You may put the sentences in any order you like.

Vince: _____

_____

Keisha: _____

_____

James: _____

_____

TRY THIS!
Talking Tip

Tell a partner about a book you have read recently. Use at least two different kinds of sentences.

A. Help Leigh write a diary entry. Look at each pair of words in parentheses. Circle the word that is spelled correctly. Then write the correct spelling of each word on the lines provided.

Saturday, March 31

    Yesterday was such a (busi   busy) day. If anyone had told me that I would be meeting a real author, I would have (laughd   laughed). I (luved   loved) every minute of it! The (faact   fact) is that even though it wasn't Mr. Henshaw, meeting Mrs. Badger was still great. I got to (esk   ask) her about Mr. Henshaw anyway. She (seys   says) he's nice, although he (dues   does) have a "wicked twinkle in his eye."

    Once Mrs. Badger called me an author, I knew I'd never (quet   quit) writing. I had lots of questions to ask her, but soon she was (gane   gone). I'm going to (wutch   watch) the school bulletin board for other writing contests to enter.

1. _____

2. _____

3. _____

4. _____

5. _____

6. _____

7. _____

8. _____

9. _____

10. _____

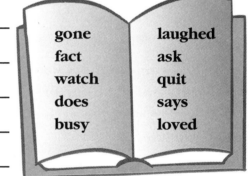

gone	laughed
fact	ask
watch	quit
does	says
busy	loved

B. Complete the unfinished word in each statement by filling in the missing letter. Then write the word on the line.

dance   switch   build   shot   health   front

1. When your body is fit, you are in good h ___ alth.   _____

2. When you do lively movement to music, you d ___ nce.   _____

3. If you get sick, you may need a sh ___ t.   _____

4. When you turn on an electric light, you use a sw ___ tch.   _____

5. When you put together materials to make a house, you b ___ ild it.   _____

6. If you are not in back, you may be in fr ___ nt.   _____

Name _____

Read each sentence and the boxed words that follow. From the box, choose a synonym for the word that appears in parentheses in the sentence. Write the synonym in the space provided.

1. I am glad Mr. Henshaw isn't the author because then I would really be (disappointed)

   _____ that I didn't get to meet him.

   | let down | happy | tired |

2. One thing was (bothering) _____ me.

   | troubling | reminding | helping |

3. I could not (locate) _____ my copy of the book.

   | open | find | remember |

4. I (searched) _____ in every room for my book.

   | walked | opened | looked |

5. Finally, when I began to get (frustrated) _____, I saw the book under a chair.

   | bored | upset | hungry |

6. Today turned out to be (thrilling) _____.

   | scary | exciting | sad |

Look at the picture, and on a separate piece of paper, make a list of words to describe it. Then exchange lists with a partner. Write synonyms for the words on your partner's list. Compare your lists.

A. Read each of the following pairs of sentences. Decide what order the events happened in, and write *first* or *second* in the space provided. Then write a sentence to explain the cause-and-effect relationship between the two events.

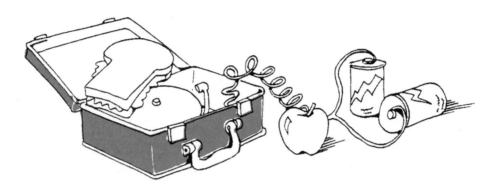

1. _____ The principal seems impressed with Leigh's invention.

   _____ Leigh has to open his lunchbox while the alarm is set.

   _____

   _____

   _____

2. _____ The winning poem is not an original work.

   _____ Angela Badger refers to Leigh as an author.

   _____

   _____

   _____

3. _____ Leigh reads *Ways to Amuse a Dog* for the "thousandth time."

   _____ Leigh's father asks him if he ever misses his "old Dad."

   _____

   _____

   _____

Name _____

B. Read the following paragraph. Then complete the cause/effect chain below.

Leigh plans to enter the Young Writers' Contest. He tries to write a mystery story about a lunchbox. It isn't very good. Then he writes a description of a day on his dad's rig. He wins an Honorable Mention and gets to meet an author. Angela Badger, the author he meets, says Leigh's description is well written and original. Leigh decides to keep writing.

Cause Leigh wants to take part in the Young Writers' Contest.	Effect Leigh decides to keep writing. _____

Effect/Cause _____ _____	Effect/Cause _____ _____

Effect/Cause _____ _____	Effect/Cause _____ _____

Effect/Cause

_____

_____

Harcourt Brace School Publishers

Using the sentence below as a model, on a separate sheet of paper, write a paragraph about a sequence of events that includes several causes and effects.

When Leigh opens his lunchbox, the lunchroom becomes very noisy.

Name _____

**Read each sentence, using context clues to determine the meaning of
the boldfaced word. Then, from the group of words that follows, circle
the one term that best completes the analogy.**

1. Worried about what his principal would say, Tim waited **anxiously** outside the office.
   Warmth is to *heat* as *anxiously* is to _____.

   coldly   joyfully   sadly   nervously

2. He tried to look **nonchalant,** but inside he was very nervous.
   Glad is to *happy* as *nonchalant* is to _____.

   concerned   careful   busy   casual

3. Tim guessed the principal would take away his recess **privileges** and make him stay inside
   during playtime.
   Student is to *pupil* as *privileges* is to _____.

   desserts   prizes   special rights   promotions

4. Everyone would make fun of him for this, and he would become a **laughingstock.**
   Piano is to *musical instrument* as *laughingstock* is to _____.

   object of ridicule   clown   darkness   sad sack

5. Tim wished he wasn't always the **culprit** responsible for creating classroom disturbances.
   Innocent is to *blameless* as *culprit* is to _____.

   crime   guilty person   lawyer   judge

6. "In trouble again, Tim?" asked a classmate **sarcastically.**
   Spin is to *turn* as *sarcastically* is to _____.

   sweetly   simply   hurtfully   kindly

Principal

Make up your own analogies for the vocabulary words, but make your clues antonyms (words with
opposite meanings) instead of synonyms (words with similar meanings). Write your analogies on index
cards, and, with a partner, take turns picking cards and solving each other's analogies.

A. Complete the chart to show the major events in "Whose Side Are You On?" and the effect each event has on Barbra.

Event	Effect on Barbra
It is report-card day.	Barbra is nervous and worried.
Barbra fails math.	
Barbra throws her report card away.	

B. What is the most important lesson you learned from the story? Why is this lesson important?

_____

_____

_____

_____

Harcourt Brace School Publishers

Name _____

A. Read this entry from Linc's diary and underline each imperative sentence.

What a rotten day this has turned out to be! I wish I could give the people around me a few rules to follow. My first rule is for parents. Don't forget to wake up your kids on time. This is especially important if your kids have forgotten to set their alarm clocks. Little sisters need to follow rules, too. First, don't ever go into your brother's room. What if he invites you? It'll never happen! Next, don't talk to your parents about your brother. Try not to talk to your brother at all. That would make everyone's life easier!

B. Read about each situation. Then write an imperative sentence you might say in that situation.

1. Your friend has your markers, and you want them back.

   _____

2. You are playing basketball, and you want a teammate to throw the ball to you.

   _____

3. You don't understand the solution to a math problem. You would like to have your teacher explain it one more time.

   _____

4. You need some help carrying a box outside. It's heavy!

   _____

5. You want to stay up later than usual to watch a special TV show.

   _____

TRY THIS! Writing

On a separate sheet of paper, write your answers to these questions.

- What are the four kinds of sentences?
- What does each kind of sentence do?
- How are all four kinds of sentences alike?

Name _____

A. Help Barbra write her thoughts about report-card day. Some words are missing a letter or letters. Fill in the missing letter or letters. Then write the word on the line provided.

nine   ray
dream   space
brain   slight
leave   tease
brief   style
straight

　　I had it for a br __ __ f time, and then my report card was gone. I hoped my br __ __ n was playing tricks on me. I felt as if I was in a dr __ __ m and would never wake up. I tried to explain to Mom what had happened, but she was supposed to l __ __ ve at n __ ne. She walked str __ __ ght out of the house before I could say a word. Later that night, I went to her room thinking I still had a sl __ ght chance. There was no sp __ ce left to hide in. I knew her st __ le. I didn't think there was even a r __ y of hope that she would understand why my report card was gone. If only T.J. didn't always try to t __ __ se me.

1. _____   5. _____   9. _____

2. _____   6. _____   10. _____

3. _____   7. _____   11. _____

4. _____   8. _____

B. Write the word from the box that names each picture.

cheese   plate
chain   cheeks
knight

1. _____   2. _____

3. _____   4. _____   5. _____

A. Read each sentence. Identify the two words or phrases from the sentence that are antonyms, and write them on the line.

1. Barbra had always been a success at school, but now she felt

   like a failure. _____

2. T. J. had been left back once because he wasn't mature enough

   to be promoted. _____

3. Barbra saw only one solution to her problem—she had to get

   rid of her report card. _____

4. Barbra had a burning feeling in her stomach that even ice-cold

   milk couldn't get rid of. _____

B. Fill in the third column of the chart with an antonym for each of the words in the first column.

Word	Synonym	Antonym
simple	easy	
gloomy	sad	
concealed	hidden	
unsure	undecided	

Think of pairs of opposite words such as *up* and *down, morning* and *night,* and so on. Play a game with a classmate. One student says a word and the partner comes up with an antonym. Continue for several turns.

Harcourt Brace School Publishers

Name _____

A. Read each of the following paragraphs. Then write a generalization about the information in the paragraph and give details to support it.

1.   At dinner, Barbra's mother announced that all her hard work had finally paid off. She was now a vice president of the bank. Her promotion would mean longer hours and more money.

Generalization: _____

_____

_____

Details to support your generalization: _____

_____

_____

2.   After the events of the day, Barbra is very quiet. Her mother wonders if she is all right. Barbra doesn't eat her food. She says she doesn't feel well just so she can be excused from the table. She decides to go to sleep to forget her troubles.

Generalization: _____

_____

_____

Details to support your generalization: _____

_____

_____

GO ON

B. Read the following paragraph. Then add details to complete the Generalization diagram below.

Barbra's mother knows something is upsetting Barbra. She tells her that whatever it is, she'll understand. Barbra finally tells her mother what happened, but her mother *doesn't* understand. In fact, she is disappointed in Barbra. She doesn't listen to Barbra's excuses, and she grounds her.

Detail		Detail		Detail
	+		+	

=
Generalization
Barbra's mother isn't sympathetic toward her.

Harcourt Brace School Publishers

TRY THIS!
Learning Log

Choose a famous person you are studying or have studied. On a separate sheet of paper, write what you know about that person. Then write a generalization about that person's life.

Whose Side Are You On?

Name _____

Read the following newspaper clipping. Then answer the questions that follow.

THE FLORIDA GAZETTE

SUNSHINE TODAY - HIGH 75°   MORNING EDITION

Good News for Fish

The Florida Game and Freshwater Fish Commission issued a statement today saying that requests for freshwater fishing licenses have decreased by 25 percent over a nine-year period. Authorities are not quite sure why there are fewer people who want to fish, but the commission is worried, since a fourth of its income comes from fishing licenses.

Some people have suggested that with other, more active things to do, fishing just isn't as popular as it once was. Others say that some children don't have anyone to go fishing with, so they never learn how. Still others argue that a great many of the people who like to fish are over 65 and don't have to buy licenses. The commission plans to conduct a study over the next five years to discover the reasons.

1. What has happened over the past nine years regarding fishing licenses in Florida?

_____

_____

2. What effect does this have on the Game and Freshwater Fish Commission?

_____

_____

3. What are some suggested causes of this decrease?

_____

_____

_____

**Read the words and their definitions on the dog house, and then
complete the analogies on the paw prints.**

1. *Losing* is to *winning* as
groveling is to _____.
standing   skipping   drawing   flying

2. *Smile* is to *happy* as
cringe is to _____.
angry   hungry   afraid   sleepy

groveling:	creeping or crawling, with the face to the ground
cringe:	to shrink back, as if in fear
propeller:	rotating blades that pull or push an aircraft or ship through air or water
pneumonia:	a disease that affects the lungs
flustered:	confused or upset

3. *Oars* are to *rowboat* as
propeller is to _____.
car   bicycle   train   airplane

4. *Cavity* is to *teeth* as
pneumonia is to _____.
brain   eyes   fingernails   lungs

5. *Calm* is to *peaceful* as
flustered is to _____.
clean   disturbed   happy   tired

TRY THIS!
Word Play

Work with a partner. Scramble the letters in each vocabulary word while your partner does the same. For
each scrambled word, write a sentence that gives a clue about what the word is. Then exchange scrambled
word lists. See who can be the first to unscramble the words.

Harcourt Brace School Publishers

Name _____

A. Summarize "Shiloh" by completing the story map.

Characters	Setting

Problem

Important Events

Solution

B. How would you describe this story to someone who has not read it?

_____

_____

_____

SUMMARIZE THE SELECTION   **19**

A. Read each sentence on the poster. Underline the complete subject, and circle the complete predicate.

LOST DOG

This cute little dog is missing.

Her name is Peaches.

Peaches has a fluffy white coat and long ears.

She weighs about twelve pounds.

We miss our friendly pet.

Anyone with information about Peaches should call Zack.

My phone number is 555-7398.

B. Finish each sentence by writing a subject or a predicate on the line. Then write *S* for subject or *P* for predicate to identify which sentence part you added.

1. The frightened puppy _____. _____

2. My friends _____. _____

3. _____ growled. _____

4. _____ dashed away. _____

5. I _____. _____

TRY THIS!
Writing

What do you think of dogs as pets? On a separate sheet of paper, write at least two declarative sentences that state your opinion. Then ask a partner to identify the subject and the predicate of each of your sentences.

Name _____

A. Shiloh wants Marty to help him. Correct the underlined words by writing the correct spelling of each word on the line provided.

bold
true
rule

soul

owe

lose
folks
clue
prove

Young human, may I be so <u>buld</u> as to tell you my <u>troo</u> story? I have no <u>foolks</u>, and my owner treats me poorly. Even if I obey every <u>roole</u>, he can <u>loose</u> patience with me. I can't seem to please him to save my <u>sul</u>. I can <u>prve</u> what I say; just look at the <u>clooes</u>. Notice my shaking and fear of people. I only come when I am called. If you will help me, I will <u>ohwe</u> my life to you.

1. _____   4. _____   7. _____

2. _____   5. _____   8. _____

3. _____   6. _____   9. _____

B. Write the word from the box that fits each description.

1. matching pants and jacket _____

2. bananas, oranges, grapes _____

3. a type of drink _____

4. used to make hair look neat _____

5. the front part of the neck under the chin _____

6. a large tree with acorns _____

7. a musical instrument _____

oak
flute
suit
fruit
comb
throat
juice

A. Read the following paragraph. Then fill in the chart below by filling in evidence to support each judgment.

After Shiloh was taken back to Judd Travers, Marty often wondered what it would be like to have a dog like Shiloh as his own. He thought about all the fun they could have together. He also worried about the dog and was afraid for him. Marty decided to raise money so he could buy Shiloh.

Valid Judgment	Evidence
Marty is a caring person.	
Marty likes dogs.	
Marty is determined.	

B. Read the following paragraph and answer the questions below.

Marty's father has trouble understanding why Marty is so concerned for Shiloh. After all, Shiloh is just a dog. While he himself would never mistreat an animal, he knows other people don't agree with his way of doing things. Marty's father doesn't want to start trouble with anybody. His motto is *Live and let live*.

1. What judgment can you make about Marty's father? _____

_____

2. What evidence do you have to support this judgment? _____

_____

3. Do you think Marty's father's motto is right or wrong? _____

_____

_____

Making judgments about characters in your reading can often help you make judgments about people in your life. In your Learning Log, write about a situation in which you or someone you know has made a judgment about a person.

Name _____

Read the following passage. Then fill in the chart below by writing details to support the generalization.

West Virginia is one of the twelve states found in the southeastern part of the United States. The Southeast is an area with many resources. Coal, oil, and natural gas are found in several of these states. There are many forests, and because much of the Southeast is bordered by water, fish are abundant.

There are areas of rich farmland throughout the Southeast. There are also mountain ranges such as the Blue Ridge Mountains. Waterways run to large ports on the Atlantic Ocean, where goods are shipped to and received from other parts of the United States. Lastly, the Mississippi River, which partly runs through the Southeast, carries freight for almost all parts of the United States between the Appalachian Mountains and the Rocky Mountains.

The Southeast and Its Resources	
Generalization The southeastern part of the United States is important to people all over the United States.	**Facts to Support**

Describe a favorite place to a partner. Have your partner make a generalization about the place you have chosen.

MAKE GENERALIZATIONS

Harcourt Brace School Publishers

Read the following paragraph. Then answer the questions below.

Did you know that you start digesting food as soon as you put it in your mouth? As you chew your food, the saliva in your mouth mixes with it, softens it, and helps you swallow it. Then the food moves through the esophagus to your stomach, where it is turned over and over. The food now combines with digestive juices in your stomach and is broken down and turned into a liquid. The liquid goes to the small intestine, where it is mixed with other digestive juices that are made in the liver and pancreas. Fats are broken down, and digestion is complete. Nutrients can get into the bloodstream and go to all of the body's cells.

1. What is the effect of putting food in your mouth?

   _____

2. What happens to the food after it goes through the esophagus?

   _____

   _____

3. What role does the small intestine play in digestion?

   _____

   _____

4. What causes nutrients to be released?

   _____

5. What happens when nutrients get into the bloodstream?

   _____

Harcourt Brace School Publishers

Name _____

**For each grouping below, read the boldfaced word and its definition.
Then follow the directions.**

1. **sift:** to pass through a strainer in order to separate fine parts from coarse parts

   a. Write your own sentence using the word *sift.*

   _____

   b. Write some things you can sift.

   _____

2. **hammock:** a bed formed from a piece of strong fabric or woven rope hung between two supports

   a. Write your own sentence using the word *hammock.*

   _____

   b. Write things you might do in a hammock.

   _____

3. **invisible:** not capable of being seen

   a. Write your own sentence using the word *invisible.*

   _____

   b. Write some things that are invisible.

   _____

4. **memorable:** hard to forget

   a. Write your own sentence using the word *memorable.*

   _____

   b. Write things that might make a day memorable.

   _____

Choose a vocabulary word, and write its letters from left to right on a chart, with one column for each letter. In each column, write words that begin with that letter. For example, if you chose the word *sift,* your first column might include *sand, soft, small,* and *silver.* Work with a partner. See who can think of more words, you or your partner.

A. Complete the outline to show what happens in "Morning Girl."

I. Morning Girl

　A. _She likes to wake up early so that she can get started before the day begins._

　B. _____

　C. _____

II. Star Boy

　A. _____

　B. _____

　C. _____

III. Morning Girl

　A. _____

　B. _____

　C. _____

B. What do you like or dislike about this story? Explain your answer.

_____

_____

_____

Name _____

A. Read this newspaper article. As shown in the first sentence, draw a vertical line to separate the complete subject and the complete predicate. Then draw one line under the simple subject and two lines under the simple predicate.

STRANGE VISITORS

Three large, strange <u>boats</u>|<u>sailed</u> toward our island this morning. The boats stopped some distance from shore. A small boat appeared in the water before long. The boat brought a group of people to our shore.

These people had bright, heavy coverings on their bodies. They spoke a strange language, too. Nobody here understood them. All my fellow islanders wonder about these strange visitors.

B. The chart below shows the simple subject and simple predicate of five sentences. Add details to both the subject and the predicate to make an interesting sentence. Write your sentences on the numbered lines.

Simple Subject	Simple Predicate
1. ships	sailed
2. sailors	arrived
3. people	watched
4. flags	fluttered
5. friends	cheered

1. _____

2. _____

3. _____

4. _____

5. _____

TRY THIS! Writing

With a partner, select a simple subject and a simple predicate for a sentence. Then take turns adding different details to create new complete subjects and predicates. See how many different sentences you can write.

Name _____

A. Morning Girl and Star Boy have different ways of seeing things. Fill in the missing letters. Then write the words on the lines provided.

round	spoil	town	noise	frown	clouds
mouth	sound	shower	moist		

Morning Girl: It is early morning, and I can hear the s __ __ nd of nature. The n __ __ se is like music to my ears. I see the cl __ __ ds coming together and feel the beginnings of a morning sh __ __ er. The m __ __ st air feels good on my m __ __ th and face.

Star Boy: Evening has finally come to this t __ __ n. The moon is not yet r __ __ nd, but it is bright. Once I see the stars, even my sister's fr __ __ n cannot sp __ __ l the night.

1. _____   5. _____   8. _____

2. _____   6. _____   9. _____

3. _____   7. _____   10. _____

4. _____

B. Which word from the box does each of the following phrases make you think of? Write that word on the line provided.

noun
proud
boil
drown
employee
employer

1. the winner of a race   _____

2. a person, place, or thing _____

3. a business owner _____

4. a sinking ship   _____

5. a pot of water   _____

6. someone who works for pay   _____

Name _____

A. Read the boxed groups of words below each sentence. Then, on the line provided, rewrite each group in order from least negative to most negative.

1. Morning Girl gave her brother a parting _____ and went outside.

look   scowl   frown

least negative _____ most negative

2. Morning Girl thinks others in her family might _____ her reasons for liking early morning.

misunderstand   misinterpret   distort

least negative _____ most negative

B. Read the boxed groups of words below each sentence. Then, on the line provided, rewrite each group in order from least positive to most positive.

1. The day _____ me with open arms.

welcomed   greeted   received

least positive _____ most positive

2. Star Boy loved the night because there were _____ things to see.

special   remarkable   memorable

least positive _____ most positive

On a separate piece of paper make a two-column chart. On one side, write positive words that describe yourself. On the other side, write synonyms that have more positive connotations than the original words have.

Harcourt Brace School Publishers

Read the following description of Star Boy. What conclusion can you draw about him from the description? What prediction can you make? Complete the chart below.

Star Boy's father gave him that name because Star Boy likes things in the night. He observes the night sky and sees a whole new world—patterns in the sky and tracks made of white sand. Star Boy has a keen awareness of his environment. He loves to use his senses, especially at night. Star Boy dreams of becoming an expert on things in the night. He knows there are things beyond the sky just waiting to be seen.

Story Evidence	What I Already Know
	People have always been interested in stars and planets. People who have good observation skills often make scientific discoveries.

Conclusion

Prediction

On a separate sheet of paper, write at least two paragraphs of a story beginning. Exchange your work with a partner. Then make up a conclusion and a prediction based on your partner's story beginning. Share your writing with your partner. You may want to use a sentence frame such as the following one to help you.

I conclude _____ because I know _____ and the paragraph said _____ .

Name _____

Read the following paragraph. Then fill in the chart to help you reach a judgment about Galileo's actions.

Scientists in the 1500s and 1600s wanted to find out more about the world. One scientist, Galileo, made his own telescope to study the sky. With his telescope, he could see the mountains and valleys of the moon and the rings of Saturn. He was able to prove that the Earth rotates on its axis. He also believed that the Earth moves around the sun and not the sun around the Earth. Many people didn't believe Galileo. They had believed other things for a long time, and they thought it was wrong to question those beliefs. Important and powerful people demanded that Galileo abandon his new ideas and stop his scientific work. Some even threatened to kill him if he didn't. Galileo finally gave in and denied his ideas, but he never really stopped believing in them. He continued his work in private. Today, we know his ideas were right.

Information from Story	**Personal Knowledge**
	• Some people are scared of change. • New ideas can make people question what they know. • Threats are often carried out.

Judgment

Talking Tip

If you were able to meet Galileo, what would you say to him about his actions?

Harcourt Brace School Publishers

Read the boldfaced vocabulary words and their definitions on the
ship's hull. Then choose the correct vocabulary word to complete each
sentence in the story that is written on the ship's sail.

Since childhood, Nathan had been fascinated by all
kinds of seagoing _____. He hoped that when
he grew up, he could join the hardworking _____
that he saw down by the docks. Nathan often made lists in
which he would _____ the amount of money he
would need to get started. He even knew how much he would
need for _____ for a voyage that would last two
months. He had read many books that explained what a
commander should do in case of a _____, but he didn't
think he'd really need that information. On the day he
_____ his own personal flag on his boat, he was a
happy man. In his first competitive race, he _____ the
prize because he was too busy having fun!

mutiny:	a rebellion against authority, especially by sailors
mariners:	sailors
vessels:	ships or boats that are larger than rowboats
provisions:	supplies, especially food
reckon:	to figure out, using arithmetic
forfeited:	lost or given up as a penalty for a mistake
unfurled:	unrolled or unfolded, as a flag

TRY THIS! Writing

On a separate piece of paper, write a diary entry that one of the sailors on Columbus's ships might have
written. Use each of the vocabulary words at least once in your diary entry. Work with a partner. Read
your diary entry to your partner, and then listen to your partner's diary entry.

Name _____

A. Summarize "The Log of Christopher Columbus" by completing the K-W-L chart.

K	W	L
What I Know	**What I Want to Know**	**What I Learned**

B. If you had been with Christopher Columbus when he landed on San Salvador, what do you think you would have talked about?

_____

_____

_____

_____

_____

_____

_____

Harcourt Brace School Publishers

Read the following pairs of sentences. Then combine each pair to make a new sentence with a compound subject or a compound predicate. Write the new sentence on the line.

Columbus tried to encourage us.
The other ships' captains tried to encourage us.

_____

_____

The Santa Maria sailed more slowly than the Pinta.
The Niña sailed more slowly than the Pinta.

_____

_____

We worried about our families.
We feared for our lives.

_____

_____

Only a few of us trusted Columbus.
Only a few of us wanted to continue.

_____

_____

TRY THIS!
Talking Tip

Tell a partner what you might have thought and done if you had sailed with Columbus. Use at least one sentence with a compound subject and at least one sentence with a compound predicate.

Name _____

The following article has been divided into two passages. First read passage A and answer the questions below it.

Two Fine Composers

A. Wolfgang Amadeus Mozart was born in Salzburg, Austria, in 1756. He was a musical genius. His father was both his teacher and his companion. Mozart began composing at age six as well as performing on the harpsichord, organ, and violin. Composing came easily to Mozart. He wrote more than 600 compositions including operas, concertos, symphonies, keyboard music, and vocal music.

Mozart was sickly and temperamental and had many bad habits. Mozart died at the young age of 35. Today, he is considered one of the greatest classical composers.

1. Which sentences or phrases give the author's opinions?

_____

_____

2. What are three facts that the author gives about Mozart?

_____

_____

_____

3. How do you know these are facts?

_____

_____

4. Would you identify the author's purpose as to inform, to entertain, or to persuade?

_____

5. How would you describe the author's viewpoint about Mozart?

_____

_____

GO ON

Name _____

Now read passage B of the article and answer the questions below.

B. Franz Joseph Haydn wrote music during the late eighteenth century—at about the same time Mozart did. In fact, the two men were friends. They probably admired and respected each other. Haydn was different from Mozart, however. He was not a genius; rather, he was patient and slow. He was not the gifted performer Mozart was, but he was a good conductor.

Haydn was employed by Prince Esterházy as the court composer, conductor, and music teacher. He had to compose whatever type of music the prince commanded. Historians have not been able to determine exactly how many compositions Haydn wrote.

1. What are three facts that the author gives about Haydn?

_____

_____

_____

2. Which sentences or phrases give the author's opinion?

_____

_____

3. What was the author's purpose in writing this article?

_____

_____

4. How does the author's viewpoint on Haydn differ from his viewpoint on Mozart?

_____

_____

TRY THIS! **Writing**

Think about one of your favorite musicians. On a separate sheet of paper, write a story about something that might have happened to that musician. Your purpose is to entertain.

Harcourt Brace School Publishers

Name _____

Read the boldfaced words and their definitions in the box below. Then complete the sentences that follow with the correct boldfaced word.

yield:	to produce; give forth
astronomy:	the science that deals with the stars, planets, and other heavenly bodies
almanacs:	yearly calendars that give facts about the weather, sun, moon, tides, and other aspects of nature
eclipses:	shadows on the earth or moon caused by other celestial bodies
unraveling:	solving, making clear, explaining
abolitionist:	doing away with something
edition:	the total number of copies of a publication printed at the same time

1. A human rights worker came to our town to talk about a new

   _____ movement.

2. The author passed out her book and said, "This is so popular that it's in its third

   _____."

3. Many farmers rely on _____ to find out when to plant their crops.

4. Water and sunlight _____ a beautiful garden.

5. You can study the heavens to learn about _____.

6. Scientists can determine when the next solar _____ will be.

7. She devoted her life to _____ the mystery of the lost settlers.

Choose a vocabulary word. If the word is a noun, write three adjectives that could be used to describe it. If the word is a verb, write three adverbs that could be used to describe it. If the word is an adjective, write three nouns it could describe.

A. Complete the chart about events in "Dear Benjamin Banneker."

Date/Time Period	Event
1731	Benjamin Banneker is born in Maryland
1789	
1790	
December 1790	
1791	
August 19, 1791	
August 30, 1791	
December 1791	
1792–1797	

B. How would you describe Benjamin Banneker to someone who has never heard of him?

_____

_____

_____

_____

_____

Harcourt Brace School Publishers

Name _____

Read the following sentences. Underline each common noun and circle each proper noun as shown. Then rewrite each sentence using different common nouns and proper nouns in place of those you have marked.

1. The young <u>scientist</u> was born in (Maryland.)

   The young dancer was born in California. _____

2. Many friends helped Benjamin Banneker.

   _____

3. People throughout the United States still recall his accomplishments.

   _____

4. Banneker helped design Washington, D.C.

   _____

5. This man had an unusually good memory.

   _____

6. The astronomer spent many nights watching the stars and planets.

   _____

7. Now, scientists are exploring Mars, Jupiter, and other planets.

   _____

8. What would Banneker think of the changes in his country?

   _____

TRY THIS!
Writing

With a partner, list ten common nouns that name people. Here are three examples: *principal, neighbor, cousin.* Then write a proper noun for each. For example: *Ms. Landers, Dr. Woo, Lettie.*

Name _____

A. Help another almanac writer finish a letter to his publisher. Find and circle the eight misspelled words in his letter. Then write the correct spelling of each word on the line provided.

Sir:

I was exsited to receive your response. I read each sentense several times to be shure I understood. Becauze of the many yearz I have struggled, I refuze to give up on my almanac. In my prezent condition and advancing age, I ask you to pleaze continue your support through the coming year.

Sincerely,

years	please
because	sure
sentence	present
refuse	excited

1. _____   4. _____   7. _____

2. _____   5. _____   8. _____

3. _____   6. _____

B. Fill in the missing letters to form a word from the box. Then write each word on the line provided.

ocean
clothes
practice
pressure
station
ancient
machine
percent

1. People say practi __ e makes perfect. _____

2. Her clothe __ were torn and worn. _____

3. He received 85 per __ ent on the test. _____

4. They sailed the o __ ean blue. _____

5. The an __ ient Egyptians built the Pyramids. _____

6. The prince's sta __ ion in life was determined before he was born. _____

7. The pres __ ure caused the explosion. _____

8. The cotton gin was a ma __ hine invented by Eli Whitney. _____

Name _____

Use the following cards from a library card catalog to answer the questions below.

A.

Black History Makers.

920   Lee, George.
Lee   Black History Makers;
      New York: McFarland
      and Co., ©1991.

AFRICAN AMERICANS

920   Lee, George.
Lee   Black History Makers;
      New York: McFarland
      and Co., ©1991.

B.

C.

920   Lee, George.
Lee   Black History Makers;
      New York: McFarland
      and Co., ©1991.

1. Which card from the card catalog is a title card? _____

2. Which card from the card catalog is an author card? _____

3. Which card from the card catalog is a subject card? _____

4. What is the call number for this title? _____

5. Who is the author of the book? _____

6. What year was the book published? _____

7. Who published the book? _____

8. If you wanted to find a book about almanacs but did not know the title or author, what could you do?

_____

_____

_____

_____

9. You want to see what books your library has on Benjamin Banneker. What can you do?

_____

_____

_____

_____

10. You enjoyed Andrea Davis Pinkney's book *Dear Benjamin Banneker*. What can you do to find out if she has written other biographies?

_____

_____

_____

_____

Knowing how to use the card catalog and understanding its contents will help you find materials quickly and easily. Suppose you wanted to find information about Thomas Jefferson. In your Learning Log, write about how you would use the card catalog to find sources.

Name _____

Read the paragraph and study the bar graph. Then answer the questions.

Marco's class has been studying weather and temperature. The students are learning to take exact temperature measurements by using a thermometer. They have kept a record of the temperature in their town over the past five days. Here is a bar graph they made showing the results.

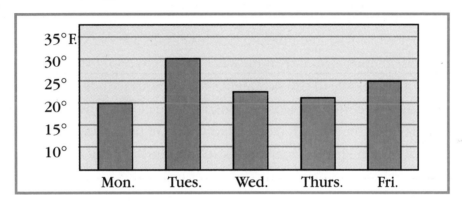

1. What conclusions can you draw about the weather over the five-day period?

_____

_____

2. On Tuesday Marco measured the temperature at 12:00 noon. On the other days he measured the temperature at 8:00 A.M. What conclusion could you draw about what the temperature readings on the other days would have been if the readings had been taken in the middle of the day?

_____

3. Do you think the results would have been more reliable if the temperature had been measured at the same time every day?

_____

_____

4. Based on the temperature over the past five days, what do you predict the temperature will be on Saturday at 8:00 A.M.? At around 12:00 noon?

_____

_____

5. What did you base your predictions on?

_____

Harcourt Brace School Publishers

Name _____

SCIENCE **Read the following paragraph. Then answer the questions below.**

Clouds come in different shapes. These shapes help us know the kind of weather we will soon be having. Stratus clouds are not very interesting to look at. These clouds form low in the sky and lead to rain. Cumulus clouds usually form in the middle of the sky, higher than stratus clouds form. Cumulus clouds look like soft cotton. When you look at these clouds, you can imagine that they look like different things. A sky filled with cumulus clouds probably means there will be no rain. Cirrus clouds are the third type of cloud. They are high in the sky, where the air is cold. The water inside these clouds is in the form of ice crystals. They are lovely and wispy and often look like feathers. Count on fair weather when you see cirrus clouds. Remember these pointers, and you'll be able to read clouds like a book.

1. What are two facts from the paragraph about each type of cloud?

    _____

    _____

    _____

2. What is one opinion from the paragraph about each type of cloud?

    _____

    _____

    _____

3. What is the author's purpose?

    _____

    _____

4. What is the author's viewpoint?

    _____

    _____

Name _____

Read the paragraph below, using context clues to determine the meaning of the boldfaced words. Then match each boldfaced word to its correct definition. Write the correct word in the space provided.

An **aviator** almost crashed his plane into this bridge once. However, he was able to land on some flat **territory** south of here. He was tracking people who were **smuggling** goods across the border. The people were in **dire** trouble because they had not paid any taxes on the goods. Now this bridge is so rickety and old that it should be **condemned.**

a region or an area _____

importing something without paying the taxes on it _____

dreadful, terrible _____

a pilot; a person who flies airplanes _____

declared unfit or unsafe for use _____

TRY THIS!
Writing

On a separate piece of paper, write word webs for each of the vocabulary words. Think of other related words to add to your webs.

A. Complete the chart about events in "Homesick: My Own Story."

Date	Event
1915	Jean is born in Hangkow, China.
1925	
1927	
May 23, 1927	
May 24, 1927	
end of May	
beginning of June	
middle of June	
2 days later	

B. Why do you think the author wrote this story? What was she trying to convey?

_____

_____

_____

_____

_____

Harcourt Brace School Publishers

Name _____

Solve this crossword puzzle. For each singular noun in the Across column, write the plural form in the puzzle. For each plural noun in the Down column, write the singular form in the puzzle.

Across

1. baby
4. tuft
6. calf
7. herd
8. story
13. dress
15. ship
17. bus
19. rehearsal
22. territory

Down

2. bushes
3. shadows
5. feet
6. children
8. shelves
9. oxen
10. sheep
11. pennies
12. passengers
14. guesses
15. scarves
16. inches
18. men
20. stars
21. lives

Writing

Look through old magazines to find pictures of people, places, and things you can label as singular or plural nouns. Cut the pictures out, and use a dark marker or pen to label them. Then paste the pictures onto a sheet of paper to make a noun collage.

Name _____

A. Help Jean finish a letter to Andrea. Correct the underlined words by writing the correct spelling of each word on the line provided.

lived   pleased   amazing   changed   walking   named   turned

watched   cried   supposed   surprised   becoming

Dear Andrea,

Our trip from California to Pennsylvania was <u>amazeing</u>. As we drove, I <u>watchied</u> the scenery change from city to country and from desert to valley. One day while my dad <u>changeed</u> a flat tire, Mom and I went <u>walkking</u> in the Ozark Mountains and picked beautiful flowers. She and I were both <u>pleassed</u> with our arrangements.

My grandmother <u>liveed</u> on a street <u>nameed</u> Shirls Avenue. This street <u>turneed</u> into a dirt road and was on a steep hill. We made it down the hill and <u>surprissed</u> my grandmother. We were <u>suppossed</u> to get there later in the week. She <u>cryed</u> tears of happiness when she saw us. It felt wonderful coming to her home and <u>becomeing</u> part of a larger family.

Your friend,

Jean

1. _____ 5. _____ 9. _____

2. _____ 6. _____ 10. _____

3. _____ 7. _____ 11. _____

4. _____ 8. _____ 12. _____

B. Two spellings are given for each word. Write the correct spelling on the line provided.

1. practicing   practiceing   _____

2. writing   writeing   _____

3. plaied   played   _____

4. teaching   teachhing   _____

played
teaching
writing
practicing

Name _____

A. Look at the list of reference sources in the box. Then read each passage below. Write the name of the best reference source or sources on the line.

a glossary   an encyclopedia   a dictionary

1. Jean's ship made a stop at the Hawaiian Islands. Where could you look to find out more about the Hawaiian Islands?   _____

2. Jean and her friend ate macaroons on the ship. Where would you look to find out what a macaroon is?   _____

3. Jean and her mother picked flowers in the Ozark Mountains. Where would you look to find a map that shows the location of these mountains?   _____

4. Jean and her mother found a plant that they named *pagoda* plant. Where would you look to find out how to pronounce *pagoda*?   _____

B. Jean read about Charles Lindbergh, the aviator, in the newspaper. You want more information about him. Answer the questions below.

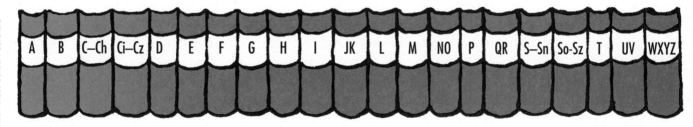

1. Which volume of the encyclopedia would you use to find out about Charles Lindbergh?

Volume _____

2. Which volume might have information about aviation? Volume _____

Harcourt Brace School Publishers

Name _____

**C. Read the following information and answer the questions about
reference sources.**

1. You find the following information on *aviator:*

   a·vi·a·tor (ā´vē·ā´tər) *n.* A person who flies airplanes or other aircraft.

   What reference source did it come from? _____

2. You are reading a book about China. In it you find this information:

   chyn: a Chinese musical instrument consisting of a board with seven strings stretched
   across it. (p. 106)

   What part of the book did this come from? _____

3. There is a photograph of Jean on the Yangtse River. You look up *Yangtse River* in the
   encyclopedia index and find this entry:

   Yangtse River. See Chang Jiang.

   What does this mean?

   _____

4. You want to do a report on China. You find this entry in the encyclopedia's index:

   > CHINA 4:329-339
   > agriculture 4:338-339
   > archaeology 2:74
   > climate 4:334
   > dance 6:9

   Where would you find information about the types of crops grown in China?

   _____

   Where would you find information about when the temperature is coldest in China?

   _____

Jean was thrilled when she sailed through the Golden Gate. In your Learning Log, write a report about the
bridge that was built across the Golden Gate. Write the steps you will follow to gather your information.
Then look up your subject and write three facts you learned about the Golden Gate Bridge.

Name _____

Think about the type of cards in a card catalog. Then answer the questions below.

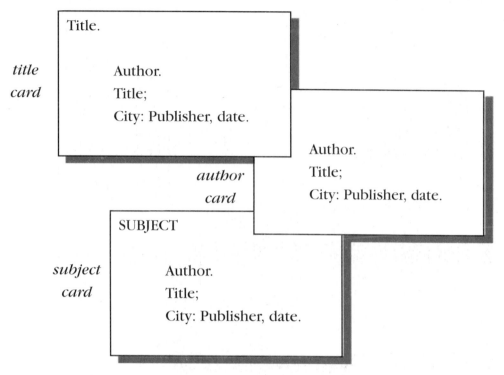

1. You want to find a book of fiction written by Jean Fritz but do not remember the title. Where could you look?

   _____

   _____

2. You are doing a report on Indians of the Great Plains states. What type of card would you use? _____

   Where else could you look? _____

3. You find the title *The Indian in the Cupboard* in a list of fiction books about Indians. You want to find out whether your library has it and who wrote it. What type of card would you use? _____

   Under what heading would you look? _____

4. After reading *The Indian in the Cupboard*, by Lynne Reid Banks, you want to read another book by the same author.
   What card would you use, and under what heading would you look? _____

   _____

Read the paragraph. Then fill in the chart below. Decide
what figure of speech each sentence or phrase is—simile,
metaphor, personification, or hyperbole. Then write the
term in the space provided.

If you attend a performance of the Metropolitan Opera in New York City,
you will see the most glorious, breathtaking sight you could imagine—a
glistening star that lights up the opera house. It is the chandelier, which rises
right before the curtain goes up. This chandelier sparkles like thousands of
diamonds. People stare and make oohing and aahing sounds. The chandelier
enjoys this attention, but it never says, "I'm too tired to go up to the ceiling
today," or "I think I'll stay and watch the opera."

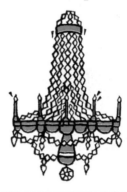

Literary Devices: Figurative Language	
	This chandelier sparkles like thousands of diamonds.
	a glistening star that lights up the opera house
	The chandelier enjoys this attention.
	the most glorious, breathtaking sight you could imagine

Talking Tip

Work with a partner. Take turns using figures of speech to describe things you might
see on a trip through the United States. For example, you might say, "The giant
redwoods in Muir Woods were so tall they could touch the stars."

Name _____

Read the boldfaced words and their definitions in the box below. Then write the words that best complete the sentences that follow.

campus:	the grounds of a school, college, or university
address:	a speech
somberly:	in a gloomy, melancholy, or sad manner
dismal:	sad and miserable
establish:	to set up on a permanent basis

1. Sarah watched a television show about the _____ lives of refugees who had been driven from their homes.

2. The narrator _____ described the hardships of life in the refugee camps.

3. As she walked across the _____ of her school, Sarah thought about this problem.

4. She decided to _____ a club to raise money to help refugees.

5. At the next assembly, Sarah made an _____ that persuaded many students to join her club.

TRY THIS! Word Play

Work in a small group. Take turns calling out a list of words that might suggest each of the vocabulary words. See who can be the first in the group to guess the word. For example, you might say, "school grounds, trees, lawns" to suggest the word *campus*. The first one to name the word is the next caller.

Harcourt Brace School Publishers

A. Summarize *Mary McLeod Bethune, Dream Maker* by completing the story map.

Scene 1

Setting: Characters:

Events:

Scene 2

Setting: Characters:

Events:

Scene 3

Setting: Characters:

Events:

B. What did you learn from this story that might help your dreams come true?

_____

_____

Name _____

A. Read each statement. Then write a short answer to the question.

1. The college president answered all the interviewers' questions.
   Were the questions asked by one interviewer or more than one interviewer?

   _____

2. The professor's diplomas hung on the wall.
   Did the diplomas belong to one professor or more than one professor?

   _____

3. The speaker's question echoed through the auditorium.
   Was the question asked by one speaker or more than one speaker?

   _____

4. Everyone could hear the students' loud response.
   Did the response come from one student or from more than one student?

   _____

5. The clubs' representatives gathered on stage.
   Were the representatives from one club or from more than one club?

   _____

B. Rewrite each phrase to include a possessive noun. The first phrase has been done for you.

the caps of the students	the students' caps
the questions of her assistant	
the notes of the secretaries	
the suggestions of one member	
the contributions of the men	
the goal of the teachers	
the hopes of the student	

TRY THIS! Writing

On a separate sheet of paper, write your answers to these questions:
   What does a possessive noun show?
   How do you form the possessive of most singular nouns?
   How do you form the possessive of plural nouns that end in *s* ?

Name _____

A. The following conversation between Mary and Rose takes place many years after the story. Find and circle the ten misspelled words. Then write the correct spelling of each word on the line provided.

opening   gathering
visiting   permitted
entered   referred
forgetting   wondering
happened   remembered

Mary: I just finished openning your telegram, and here you are! I'm so glad you are visitting.

Rose: I'm happy that you rememberred me.

Mary: I don't make a habit of forgeting people. In fact, I've thought of you often and was curious about what had happenned to you.

Rose: I've spent several years gatherring information for a book. I hope to write it over the next few years while I work at something else.

Mary: How wonderful that you have enterred the world of writing.

Rose: I was wonderring if you had any teaching positions open. I would like to be permited to share my knowledge with young people.

Mary: How fortunate! Many new students have been refered to us, and we need another teacher. You may have the job.

1. _____   6. _____

2. _____   7. _____

3. _____   8. _____

4. _____   9. _____

5. _____   10. _____

B. Each underlined word below is missing an *-ed* or an *-ing*. Determine the correct ending. Then write the whole word on the line provided.

1. She became <u>fluster</u> by all the reporter's questions. _____

2. They traveled by <u>cover</u> wagon out west. _____

3. The soldiers were <u>order</u> to turn back. _____

4. She <u>regret</u> her decision not to go to college. _____

5. Many people have <u>suffer</u> at the hands of tyrants. _____

6. He <u>control</u> his temper much better. _____

covered
ordered
regretted
suffered
controlled
flustered

Name _____

Read the drama terms in the box below. Then fill in the blanks in the paragraph that follows with the correct terms from the box.

stage directions	cast of characters	downstage	scenes

performance   acts   setting   upstage

Did you know that plays are divided into _____ and

_____? Each scene may occur in a different

_____, or the entire action of the play may take place in

one location. Each member of the _____ has a specific

role to play in moving the plot of the play along. Included as part of a play

are _____. These tell where and when the characters

move. In a live _____ of a play, characters move

_____, which is toward the back of the stage, and

_____, which is toward the front of the stage.

TRY THIS! Writing

With a partner, make a poster advertising a performance of "Mary McLeod Bethune, Dream Maker." Use several drama terms in your poster.

Harcourt Brace School Publishers

Read the following story. Then fill in the story map on the next page.

CAST LIST

Sarah wondered what to do now. She had just found out that she hadn't gotten the part she wanted in the school play. She was embarrassed. She had already bragged to everyone about how great she was going to be in the part. To make matters even worse, her mother had let her take acting lessons so that she would be ready to do the play. Sarah had dreamed of becoming an actor. Now everything was ruined.

As soon as she walked in the door, her mother hugged her and asked, "So how does it feel to be the star of the play?" Sarah said, "They canceled the play. Now I'll never be an actor." Then she went to her room. Later she would tell her mother the truth. For now, she just wanted to think.

At dinner, Sarah's parents talked about their day and then asked Sarah about the play. Before Sarah told them the truth about what had happened, she said, "I want to quit acting lessons. I'll never be an actor." Then she told them that she hadn't been picked for the play. Her parents said they were sorry about the part but explained that nobody should give up a dream just because of one small setback. Her father said, "There will be other plays and other places to begin your acting career. You must keep trying."

The next day at acting class, Sarah's drama coach told her about a theater group that would be having auditions the following week. He suggested that Sarah try out for a part. At first Sarah was reluctant. Then she thought to herself, Maybe my dream can still come true.

HISTORY

SARAH

Name _____

Characters	Setting

Plot

Theme

Harcourt Brace School Publishers

Make a plan for a story you would like to write. In your Learning Log, draw a story map showing characters, setting, plot, and theme.

Name _____

A. Read the names of the reference sources in the box. Choose the one that best completes each sentence below. Write it on the line provided.

a dictionary   a glossary   an encyclopedia

1. To find out how to pronounce *entrepreneur*, you would look in _____

   or _____.

2. If you wanted to find information about the playwright William Shakespeare, you would

   use _____.

3. To find out the part of speech for the word *improvise*, you would look in

   _____ or _____.

B. Read the following part of an encyclopedia article. Then answer the questions below.

> **drama**   from the Greek verb *dran*, meaning "to act" or "to do." It refers to actions or deeds as they are performed in a theatrical setting for an audience. *See also* THEATER, OPERA, DANCE.

1. What related articles are cross-referenced in the article about drama?

   _____

2. If you did not know the meaning of the word *theatrical* as it is used in the article, where

   could you find out what it means?_____

3. What language does the word *drama* come from? _____

4. Think of a subject that interests you. How could an encyclopedia and a dictionary help
   you find out more about the subject?

   _____

   _____

   _____

Name _____

Read the paragraph below, using context clues to determine the meaning of each boldfaced word. Write the correct boldfaced word next to its definition. Then write a paragraph of your own using the vocabulary words.

Justin **scoured** the paper, looking for something to do on a Saturday. He saw an ad for a helicopter ride in return for a $5 **donation** to the animal shelter.

Driving to the airport, he **maneuvered** his way through traffic. While in the air, he tried to pick out a few **landmarks** on the ground. From his height, the green of the lakes below looked like a strange chemical **concoction.**

1. went through every part of, as in making a search _____

2. something made by mixing ingredients _____

3. a gift or contribution _____

4. moved skillfully _____

5. familiar or outstanding objects in a landscape _____

_____

_____

_____

_____

_____

TRY THIS! Word Play

Play this with a partner. While one of you acts out a vocabulary word, the other guesses what the word is. Take turns.

Harcourt Brace School Publishers

Name _____

A. Complete the story map about "Nickel-a-Pound Plane Ride."

Main Characters	Setting

Problem

Important Events

Solution

B. What message did you learn from this story?

_____

_____

_____

_____

Name _____

Read the following sentence pairs. Circle the pronoun in the second sentence of each pair. Then underline the antecedent of that pronoun.

1. A glider soars through the air. It must be pulled up by an airplane.

2. My aunt is an airline pilot. She has been flying for more than twenty years!

3. Seaplanes have floats instead of wheels. They land and take off on water.

4. Hello, my name is Junie. I think all kinds of planes are fascinating!

5. In most planes, the pilot and copilot sit together in the cockpit. The instruments there guide them in flying the plane.

6. My brother and I both like to fly. We might become pilots.

7. Look up there, Donnie. Do you see the skywriting?

8. Some planes do special kinds of jobs. For example, they can be used to spray crops.

9. In 1903 Orville Wright became the first airplane pilot. He stayed in the air for twelve seconds.

TRY THIS! Talking Tip

Tell a partner about a type of aircraft you find interesting. Use at least three pronouns, and be sure each pronoun has a clear antecedent.

Name _____

A. Have you ever wanted to fly as Araceli did? Find and circle the eight misspelled words. Then write the correct spelling of each word on the line provided.

Would you rathur be in a large plane or a small plane for your first flight? We have more than a dozun planes to choose from. During takeoff, you may become frozin with fear, but that will pass quickly. You'll burst a butten with pride when you see the beautiful sights of our community, including a canyun, a mountain, and lakes. You wouldn't be humin if you didn't experience a slight sense of terrer as the plane starts to drop. Fear is never a facter for your pilot, however; he or she will bring you back safely.

human
dozen
frozen
factor
canyon
rather
terror
button

1. _____   4. _____   7. _____

2. _____   5. _____   8. _____

3. _____   6. _____

B. Add the correct endings to complete the words from the box. Write the word on the line.

dragon
tower
flavor
chapter
oven
daughter
woman
odor

1. drag___ ___   _____

2. wom___ ___   _____

3. daught___ ___   _____

4. ov___ ___   _____

5. chapt___ ___   _____

6. od___ ___   _____

7. tow___ ___   _____

8. flav___ ___   _____

Name _____

A. Study the map. Then answer the questions below.

1. What city lies northeast of Oakland?

_____

2. If you were in Bakersfield, in what direction would you travel to get to the Mojave Desert?

_____

3. Araceli lives somewhere in the San Joaquin Valley near Fresno. Does she live closer to Death Valley or to the Cascade Mountains?

_____

4. About how far is Fresno from Death Valley?

_____

150 miles

★ Capitol   ⋀⋀ Mountains

■ Cities   Deserts

Valleys

B. Look at the following time line. Then answer the questions on the next page.

Events in California's History

1542	1840s	1848	1850	1906
Juan Cabrillo visits San Diego Bay	John Sutter and others help develop towns	Gold found in northern California; thousands of people head west	California becomes the thirty-first state	Earthquake and fire destroy nearly all of San Francisco

GO ON

Name _____

1. What happened in 1848 that might have led to California's becoming a state?

   _____

   _____

2. When did California become a state? _____

3. With what year does the time line begin? _____

   With what year does it end? _____

4. What happened in San Francisco in 1906?

   _____

   _____

C. **Study the following table. Then answer the questions below.**

Selected Cities in California: 1990 Census Populations

City	Population
Anaheim	266,406
Beverly Hills	31,971
Fresno	667,490
Los Angeles	8,863,164
San Diego	2,498,016

1. How many people lived in San Diego in 1990? _____

2. How many more people lived in Los Angeles than in San Diego? _____

3. Which city had the lowest population? _____

TRY THIS! Learning Log

Look through newspapers or magazines and find articles with graphic aids such as maps, charts, tables, and time lines. In your Learning Log, write how graphic aids help you understand the articles.

Name _____

Look at the reference sources named in the box. Then read each item of information. Write the name of the reference source or sources where you would probably find the information.

SCIENCE

a dictionary   a glossary   an encyclopedia

1. synonyms for the word *aviator*

   _____

2. history of space flight

   _____

3. photograph of men landing on the moon

   _____

4. names of famous astronauts

   _____

5. word histories for the names of the planets

   _____

6. distances of planets from the sun

   _____

TRY THIS!
Game

Work with a partner. Research the subject of flying in several reference sources. Make a list of all the reference sources you used and what information you gathered from each.

**P.E./
HEALTH**

**Read the following paragraph. Then answer the
questions below.**

Denny had a major English test this morning. He
was so worried that he couldn't eat breakfast. He
studied instead. The test was given just before lunch,
and Denny was feeling hungry. He had trouble with
the first question, even though it was one he had
studied just before he left for school. During recess,
Denny's friend asked how he had done on the test.
Denny snapped that it was none of his business.

1. Who is the main character? _____

2. What is the setting of the story? _____

3. What happens in the story?

   _____

   _____

   _____

4. What do you think Denny's main problem is?

   _____

5. How do you think his problem could have been avoided?

   _____

6. Underline the sentence you think best states the theme.

   a. Students who study do well on tests.

   b. It is important to take care of all your needs.

   c. Eating is more important than studying.

**TRY
THIS!**
Talking Tip

Choose a favorite story or fairy tale. Tell a friend about the characters, plot, setting,
and theme.

Harcourt Brace School Publishers

Name _____

Read the boldfaced words and their definitions in the box below. Then complete each sentence that follows with the correct vocabulary word.

turbulence:	irregular movement or disturbance in a liquid or a gas
indicate:	to give signs of
static:	electrical interference picked up by a radio or a TV set; noise
transmission:	a message sent out by means of electricity or electromagnetic waves
vague:	not definite or clear
abated:	became less in force or intensity
visualize:	to see in one's mind

1. In her most recent radio _____, the pilot said that she was experiencing bad weather.

2. The air _____ jarred the plane, causing some of the passengers to worry.

3. "Does this bumpy ride _____ mechanical problems?" one of them asked.

4. The _____ on the radio made it hard for the pilot to hear instructions from the ground.

5. The passengers began to _____ the worst, but the pilot had everything under control.

6. She soon saw the shadowy, _____ outlines of the city below.

7. The tension everyone was feeling slowly _____, and they breathed more easily.

Word Play

Write each vocabulary word on a separate index card. For each word, write a synonym or a brief definition on another index card. Mix up all the cards, and place them face down. With a partner, take turns turning a card over and trying to find its match. If you are successful, keep the pair and take another turn. If you fail to make a match, play passes to your partner. The one with more pairs at the end is the winner.

A. Complete the sequence chart to summarize "Hatchet."

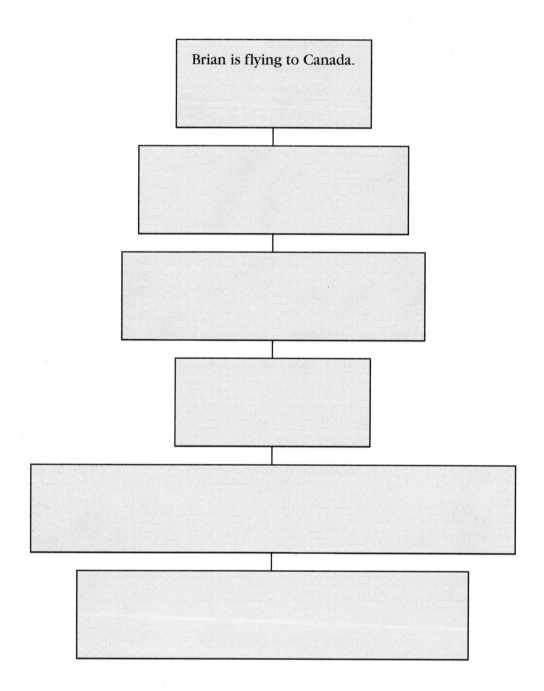

Brian is flying to Canada.

B. Which part of this story impressed you the most? Give reasons for your answer.

_____

_____

_____

Harcourt Brace School Publishers

Name _____

A. Add a pronoun to complete each sentence. The words in parentheses tell you what kind of pronoun to add and what word is its antecedent.

1. Darya's dream was to see _____ own name in the record books. (possessive pronoun—Darya)

2. _____ flew a small plane from coast to coast. (subject pronoun—Darya)

3. Did anyone help _____ fly the plane? (object pronoun—Darya)

4. No, she had to fly it by _____. (reflexive pronoun—Darya)

5. Mr. Mendez let Darya fly _____ plane. (possessive pronoun—Mr. Mendez)

6. Several reporters interviewed Darya, and _____ stories were reprinted in Darya's hometown newspaper. (possessive pronoun — reporters)

7. Darya's classmates read the news stories, and some of _____ wished they could fly, too. (object pronoun—classmates)

8. Darya told her friends, "The flight was terrific, but _____ am glad to be home." (subject pronoun—Darya)

B. Write your own sentences about flying.

1. Use the reflexive pronoun *myself.*

_____

2. Use the subject pronoun *we.*

_____

3. Use the object pronoun *them.*

_____

On a separate sheet of paper, write your answers to these questions:
   What are the singular reflexive pronouns?
   What are the plural reflexive pronouns?
   Which possessive pronouns are used alone, without a noun following them?

Harcourt Brace School Publishers

A. The words below are missing their endings. Find the word in the plane that fits each group of letters. Write the whole word on the line.

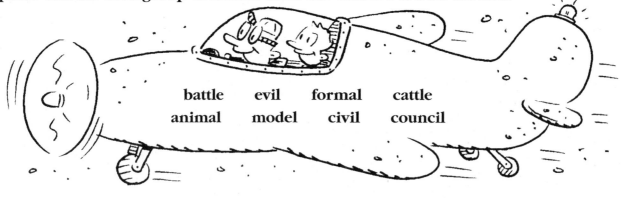

battle   evil   formal   cattle
animal   model   civil   council

1. ev __ __   _____

2. counc __ __   _____

3. anim __ __   _____

4. mod __ __   _____

5. batt __ __   _____

6. catt __ __   _____

7. form __ __   _____

8. civ __ __   _____

B. How might the story have been different if Brian had been able to have radio contact? Circle the spelling errors, and write the correct spelling of each word on the line provided.

| simple | metal | level | single | double | couple | trial | needle |

Brian: Help! Flying this plane is not simpel. There are definitely more than a coupel of

things I need to know. Over. _____, _____

Radio: Yes, there sure are. First, at what leval are you? Which number is the first

needel pointing to? Over. _____, _____

Brian: It's hard to tell. I guess 5,000. I think we're going to have to do this by triel and error.

Over. _____

Radio: Okay. Now look for the singal gauge and the doubel gauge. Tell me what they say.

Over. _____, _____

Brian: Hey, wait a minute. There's an open space ahead. Just tell me how to set this metel

thing down. Hurry. Over. _____

Name _____

Read the paragraph below using context clues to determine the meanings of the underlined words. Then match each underlined word with its definition.

Jeannine took her place in the cockpit of the plane. She was ready for her lesson. She checked to make sure that the wing flaps were working so the plane could get off the ground. She also checked the rest of the plane—the tail and the fuselage. Before the airplane left the hangar, Jeannine made sure the logbook was in place so she could keep a record of the flight. Today Jeannine was going to learn how to use the altimeter so she could tell how high she was flying. This was going to be a great lesson!

1. _____ the part of an airplane that does not include the wings and the tail

2. _____ a book found in an airplane, used to record flight information

3. _____ surfaces on the edges of the wings that move and help the plane take off and land

4. _____ an instrument used to measure height

5. _____ the place in an airplane where the pilot and other crew members sit

6. _____ a place where planes are stored

Suppose you were taking your first airplane ride. On a separate piece of paper, make a list of words that describe what you might feel.

Read the following paragraph. Then fill in the story map below.

Dawn rode her bicycle to school, enjoying the cool morning. When she arrived, she noticed that there were no other bicycles on the bicycle rack. I must be a little early, she thought. She walked up to the door and pushed, but it wouldn't open. It seemed to be locked. Dawn looked inside and saw the janitor. He came to the door chuckling and reminded Dawn that there was no school on Saturdays. As she rode her bicycle back home, Dawn decided to check her calendar more often.

Characters	Setting

Plot

Theme

Work with a partner to plan a sequel to the story. Include what happens after Dawn gets back home. On a separate sheet of paper, create a story map for the sequel.

Name _____

Look at the following map. Use it to answer the questions on the following page.

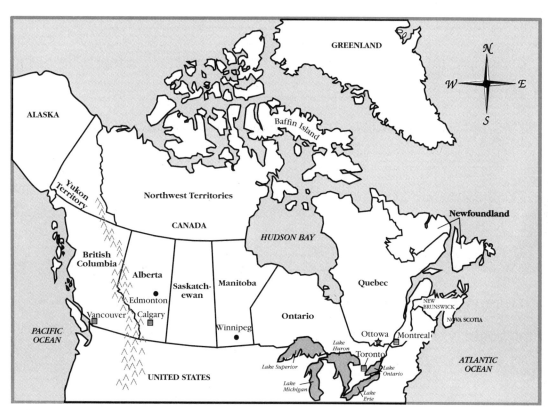

Name _____

1. What does the map show?

   _____

2. Why is there a compass rose on the map? _____

3. What does the legend explain? _____

4. You are in Vancouver, and you want to travel to Edmonton. In which direction will you go?

   _____

5. You are in the Yukon Territory. What state of the United States is northwest of there?

   _____

6. Which ocean borders the provinces of Newfoundland and Nova Scotia?

   _____

   Which ocean borders British Columbia? _____

7. You are in the province of Ontario. You want to travel to Baffin Island. Which body of

   water will you probably cross? _____

8. About how far is it from Montreal to Calgary? _____

9. Which Great Lakes are in both Canada and the United States?

   _____

10. You are traveling west from Winnipeg. In what city might you end up?

   _____

On a separate sheet of paper, draw a map of your school or town. Include a compass rose and a legend. Write three questions that can be answered by using the map.

Name _____

Read each sentence or group of sentences using context clues to determine the meaning of the boldfaced word. Circle the word below that is closest in meaning to the boldfaced word.

1. Paulette's Parrot Shop sells parrots **exclusively.** There are no other kinds of birds in the store.

   cheaply   only   reluctantly   quickly

2. Paulette says that it's very difficult to sell a **mute** parrot. People buy parrots to hear them talk.

   silent   noisy   musical   colorful

3. If a parrot doesn't want to talk, there is no way you can **blackmail** it into talking. Birds don't understand that type of force.

   reward   teach   entertain   threaten

4. Once Paulette advertised her store on the radio. The **broadcaster** made a special announcement every hour.

   salesperson   secretary   veterinarian   announcer

5. Listeners were calling and asking for talking birds. Paulette kept **evading** the questions, since the birds were not yet trained to talk.

   answering   asking   avoiding   rewording

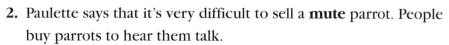
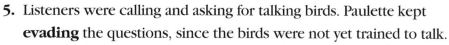

TRY THIS! Writing

Work with a partner. Imagine that you are radio announcers. Write a news story about upcoming school events that you would announce during a morning broadcast at school. Use all the boldfaced words. Share your story with another pair of students.

Name _____

A. Complete the problem-solution chart about "Radio Fifth Grade."

Problem	Solution
The parrot won't talk.	
The parrot has the hiccups.	
The parrot topples over in a dead faint.	

B. Describe the part of this story that you found the funniest.

_____

_____

_____

_____

_____

Name _____

A. Circle the adjective in each sentence. Do not mark the articles.

1. They used sturdy wood to build the house so that it would not fall down.

2. On her birthday Julie's parents bought her a fluffy rabbit.

3. The excited girls could not sleep on Christmas Eve.

4. The silent classroom was suddenly filled with children.

5. Mrs. Smith's class had five fish in an aquarium.

6. All students must do homework.

7. Tim's mom did not like the noisy music Tim listened to.

8. In the band there was one boy who played the trumpet.

9. Cindy's telephone had a long cord so she could walk around when
   she was on the phone.

10. The team liked to play outside on the green grass instead of inside the gym.

11. Our cat has soft fur and loves to play with yarn.

12. Tom lifted the heavy bat and swung at the baseball.

B. Complete the following paragraph by writing an adjective on each line. Then underline each article in the paragraph.

Tyrone pushed open the _____ door and stepped into the

_____ pet shop. _____ wall was lined with

_____ cages, and each cage held a _____,

_____ puppy. _____ the puppies were barking excitedly.

In the middle of the shop, _____ parrots sat on their perches. They were all

bright _____, and they were all squawking. Most of the noise came from an

area at the back, however. There, a group of _____ children had gathered

around the glass case that held a long, _____ snake.

Try This!
Talking Tip

Tell a partner about the most unusual pet you can imagine. Use adjectives to help your partner see and
hear that pet.

A. Improve these radio advertisements. Decide which of the two spellings of each pair in parentheses is correct, and circle it.

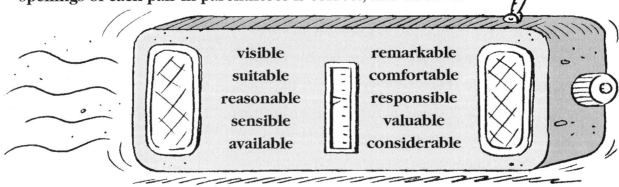

visible
suitable
reasonable
sensible
available

remarkable
comfortable
responsible
valuable
considerable

Are you (comfortible comfortable) with your exercise program? Do you want to find a program that is more (suitible suitable) for you? A combination of (sensable sensible) exercise and good eating habits will help you reach your peak of fitness. You will notice a (visable visible) difference in several weeks. Sign up today and get in shape the (responsable responsible) way.

Have you gone to (considerible considerable) expense to keep your pet happy and healthy? How do you protect your (valuable valuible) animals? Find out about our new and (remarkeble remarkable) insurance program for pets. We insure any and all animals. We offer (reasonible reasonable) payments on a monthly basis. To find out what kind of policy is (availeble available) for your pet, contact us today.

B. The words below are all missing the suffix *-ible* or *-able*. For each word, decide which suffix is correct. Then write the word on the line provided.

| capable | terrible | favorable |
| horrible | miserable | probable |

1. cap _____   4. terr _____

2. prob _____   5. favor _____

3. miser _____ 6. horr _____

Name _____

A. Read the following two descriptions. Then complete the Venn diagram below to compare and contrast the clubs.

The Amateur Radio Club invites all students of Randall Middle School to join the club. Club members believe that radio is an excellent form of entertainment. The club's main purpose is to find out about and listen to radio broadcasts of the past and present. The members also listen to a different station every week and review the programs in the school newspaper. Sometimes they write radio scripts and do imaginary radio shows.

The Radio Broadcasters' Club wants new members. Club members are convinced that radio broadcasts can provide excellent entertainment. The club's main purpose is to broadcast a radio show once a week. The show deals with current topics important to young people. The members write their own scripts. They like trying different formats on their show, and they often invite a teenage guest.

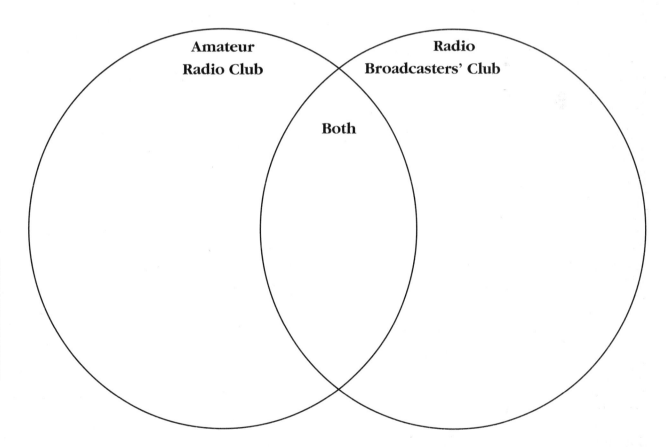

GO ON

B. Read the following paragraph. Then complete the Venn diagram below.

Birds and reptiles are two branches within the animal kingdom. Both are vertebrates, or animals with backbones. Birds have feathers and are warm-blooded. Reptiles are cold-blooded and have scales covering their body. Birds have no teeth, so they eat seeds, fruit, insects, fish, and some meat. Many reptiles can swallow food larger than they themselves are. Birds have hollow bones, and they lay eggs. Reptiles have strong bones and well-developed lungs. Some also lay eggs.

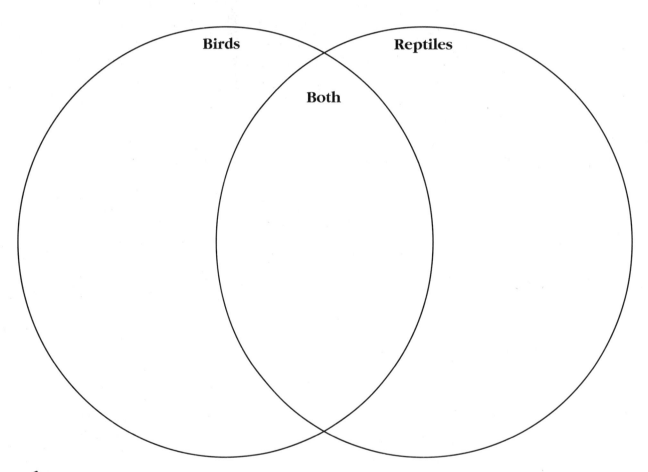

Birds

Reptiles

Both

TRY THIS! Writing

Knowing how to compare and contrast may help you make judgments about what you read. On a separate sheet of paper, write the headings *Likenesses* and *Differences*. Compare and contrast two objects or activities, such as dancing and football or a ball and a jump rope.

Name _____

Read the boldfaced words and their definitions in the box below. What related words come to your mind? Create a web of related words for each boldfaced word. An example has been done for you.

impose:	to force
stragglers:	persons who lag behind a group
influence:	power over others
truce:	a temporary stop, by mutual agreement, in fighting
violated:	broke a rule or an agreement
neutrality:	not taking sides, as in a war

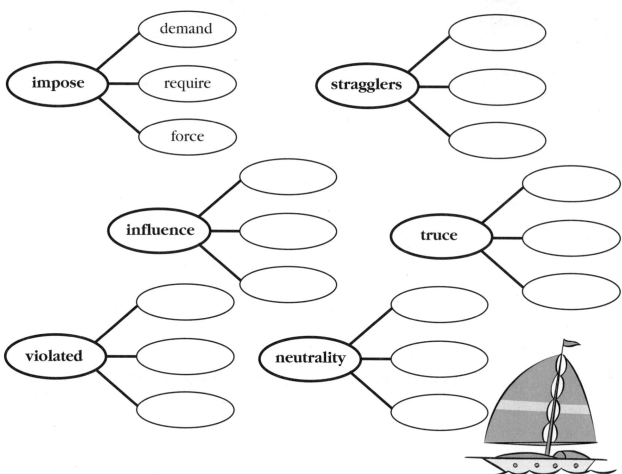

Work with a partner to write a newspaper story about a political event. The story may be a real one or one you make up. Use all the vocabulary words in your story.

A. Summarize "By the Dawn's Early Light" by completing the K-W-L chart.

K	W	L
What I Know	**What I Want to Know**	**What I Learned**

B. Suppose you had been around during the time of Francis Scott Key. What might you have said about his song?

_____

_____

_____

_____

_____

Harcourt Brace School Publishers

Name _____

**Look at each picture. Then write a proper adjective to complete the
sentence that goes with the picture. (If you need help spelling the
proper adjectives, look them up in a dictionary.)**

This is an _____ flag.

This is a _____ newspaper.

This is _____ cloth.

This is a _____ gem.

This is a _____ wall.

These are _____ pyramids.

This is a _____ mountain.

This is a _____ skater.

TRY THIS!
Talking Tip

With a partner, discuss foods of other countries. Use proper adjectives in your discussion.

A. Help Samuel Sands, a young apprentice printer. While he was setting the type for a handbill, he dropped the letters on the floor. Complete each word by adding the correct suffix. Then write the whole word on the line provided.

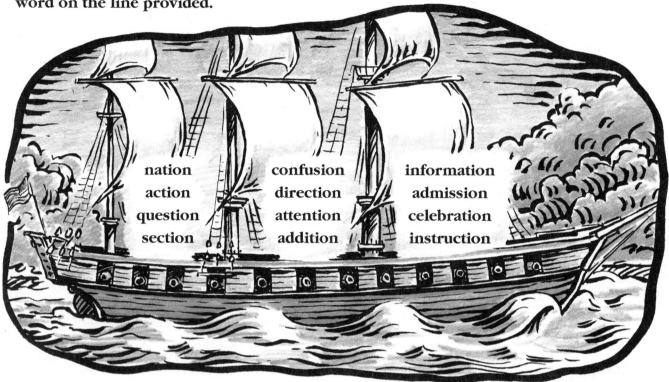

nation
action
question
section

confusion
direction
attention
addition

information
admission
celebration
instruction

1. celebra __ __ __ __ _____

2. direc __ __ __ __ _____

3. na __ __ __ __ _____

4. ac __ __ __ __ _____

5. confu __ __ __ __ _____

6. informa __ __ __ __ _____

7. instruc __ __ __ __ _____

8. admis __ __ __ __ _____

9. ques __ __ __ __ _____

10. atten __ __ __ __ _____

11. sec __ __ __ __ _____

12. addi __ __ __ __ _____

B. Unscramble each group of letters to form a word from the box. Write the word on the line provided.

| education | vacation | permission | television |

1. ctvaiona _____

2. nedoiucat _____

3. iontelvise _____

4. spieornmsi _____

Name _____

A. Read each word and the two meanings given for it. Then use context clues to determine which meaning fits the underlined word in the sentences that follow. Write the correct meaning on the line.

Word	Meanings
land	the solid, exposed surface of the earth to arrive or cause to arrive
mouth	the part of a body of water where it enters a larger body of water the opening through which food is taken into the body
retreat	a quiet refuge to go back; to withdraw
dawn	the first appearance of light in the morning to begin to appear or develop
hail	drops of ice that fall during a storm an exclamation of greeting or tribute
hold	to keep confined to regard or consider
line	a boundary or border a row

1. With the glimmer of <u>dawn</u> on the horizon, the sailors prepared the ship for casting off.

   In the sentence, *dawn* means _____

2. The <u>mouth</u> of the river is situated on the Atlantic Ocean.

   In the sentence, *mouth* means _____

   _____

3. As the general passed by, the soldiers cheered, "<u>Hail</u> to our leader!"

   In the sentence, *hail* means _____

Harcourt Brace School Publishers

4. The British fleet was forced to <u>retreat</u>.

In the sentence, *retreat* means _____

5. The <u>line</u> dividing the two countries was clearly noted on the map.

In the sentence, *line* means _____

6. The War of 1812 was fought on both water and <u>land</u>.

In the sentence, *land* means _____

7. The British officers made sure to <u>hold</u> Francis Scott Key and the others on the ship until

the battle was over.

In the sentence, *hold* means _____

**B. Read the following meanings for the word *tune*. Then write two
sentences, using a different meaning of *tune* in each.**

tune   1. a melody, usually simple and easy to remember 2. being at the proper pitch
3. one's attitude or approach

_____

_____

_____

_____

_____

_____

Learning Log

Using context clues can help you determine which meaning of a word is intended. In your Learning Log,
explain how a diagram such as the following could help you figure out the intended meanings of words
in a story.

possible meanings + context clues = intended meaning of word

Harcourt Brace School Publishers

Name _____

Read the paragraphs. Then complete the Venn diagram.

The flute and the piccolo are musical instruments in the woodwind family. Both are played by blowing across the mouthpiece, which is on the side of the instrument. The air enters the instrument, vibrates, and makes the sound. Different sounds are made by opening and closing keys. Both flutes and piccolos are made in sections, which the player fits together. Most flutes and piccolos are made of metal.

The clarinet is another member of the woodwind family. It has a bell-shaped opening at one end and a mouthpiece with a reed attached at the other end. The clarinet is made of a cylindrical tube of wood, and like the flute and the piccolo, it comes in sections. The player produces sound by breathing into the mouthpiece, which causes the reed to vibrate. Different sounds are formed by opening and closing keys.

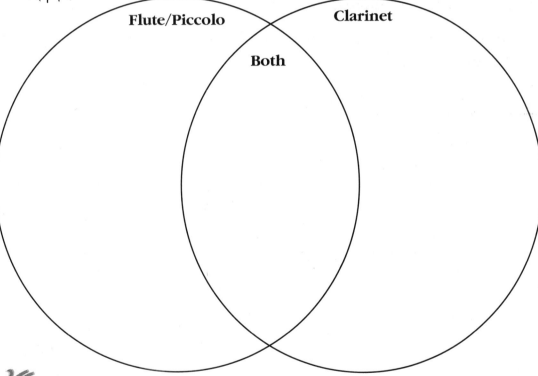

Flute/Piccolo   Clarinet

Both

Work with a partner. Gather information about an instrument of the orchestra. Then discuss your instrument with another pair of students who have gathered information about a different instrument. Compare and contrast the instruments in your discussion.

Name _____

Read what each character is saying, and try to determine the meanings of the boldfaced words from context clues. Then circle the word that best completes the analogy.

1. I gave my first piano **recital** when I was seven years old. Performing in public was scary.
   Test is to *study* as *recital* is to _____.
   character   plot   song   practice

2. I get **stage fright** before every performance, and I try to control it by remembering that I have practiced the songs well.
   Applauding is to *booing* as *stage fright* is to _____.
   fear   confidence   attractiveness   nervous

3. This **quartet** is the best musical group I've ever played with. We're thinking of adding a fifth player, but we might stick with four.
   Trio is to *three* as *quartet* is to _____.
   four   two   crowd   group

4. After the show, we're serving sandwiches to the audience. I **kneaded** the dough for the bread myself.
   Stirred is to *sauce* as *kneaded* is to _____.
   dough   ate   sliced   cooked

TRY THIS!
Writing

Think about a time you performed in front of an audience or a time you watched a performance. Write the beginning of a story about it, using all the vocabulary words. Work with a partner. Read your story beginning to your partner. Then ask your partner what he or she thinks happened next. Trade stories, and finish each other's stories in an imaginative way.

Name _____

A. Complete the story map about "Yang the Youngest and His Terrible Ear."

Characters	Setting

⬇ ⬇

Problem

⬇

Important Events

⬇

Solution

B. What is the most important message you learned from the story?

_____

_____

_____

Harcourt Brace School Publishers

Name _____

Look at the pictures. Then write your own sentences.

| violin | viola | cello | bass viol | kettledrum |

1. Compare the violin and the cello. Use a form of the adjective *big*.

   _____

2. Compare the sizes of all four of the stringed instruments. Use a form of the adjective *large*.

   _____

3. Compare the sound of the violin and the sound of the kettledrum.
   Use a form of the adjective *loud*.

   _____

4. Compare the sound of most classical music to that of most country music. Use a form of the adjective *quiet*.

   _____

5. Compare all the instruments in the pictures. Use a form of the adjective *small*.

   _____

6. Compare the sound of the cello and the sound of the kettledrum.
   Use a form of the adjective *good*.

   _____

TRY THIS!
Talking Tip

Tell a partner about some of the musical instruments you like or dislike. Use at least two adjectives that compare.

Name _____

A. Yang is thinking aloud. The underlined words are misspelled. Write the correct spelling of each one on the line provided.

produce

prepare

protect

pretend

previous

predict

process

precaution

product

prefer

program

promised

It's awful to be part of a musical family and have to <u>pertend</u> I know how to play. I always dread every <u>porgram</u>. I <u>perfer</u> playing sports or drawing to performing. But I <u>pormised</u> I would try. I just had to <u>perpare</u> myself for the worst. It is a <u>porcess</u> I go through. I know people expect the end <u>porduct</u> to be musical. I can always <u>perdict</u> their disappointment. But this time is going to be different. To <u>portect</u> myself from embarrassment, I have taken a special <u>percaution</u>. I have asked a friend to play from behind the curtain that I am going to sit in front of. I will move as if I am playing; he will <u>porduce</u> the sounds. I don't know why I didn't think of this for <u>pervious</u> programs!

1. _____   5. _____   9. _____

2. _____   6. _____   10. _____

3. _____   7. _____   11. _____

4. _____   8. _____   12. _____

B. Find the missing *pre-* or *pro-* prefix. For each incomplete word, decide which prefix is needed. Then write the word on the line provided.

preview
prevent
provide
project

1. _ _ _ ject   _____

2. _ _ _ view   _____

3. _ _ _ vent   _____

4. _ _ _ vide   _____

Name _____

Read each paragraph. Then answer the questions that follow it.

Mark loves playing the bass drum. He believes the bass drum is the key marching-band instrument. The rest of the band members agree. They hear its steady beat and are able to march and play together. Mark is proud to carry and play his bass drum in the band.

1. Which point of view is used—first person, third-person limited, or third-person

   omniscient? _____

2. How do you know this? _____

   _____

3. Rewrite the paragraph using a different point of view. Indicate which point of view you

   have used. _____

   _____

   _____

   _____

   _____

Melanie was the only one in her family who seemed unable to draw. I can't even draw a simple picture of a house. It really bothered Melanie, too, especially when Kevin, the "baby," drew great pictures. Kevin knew it upset Melanie, but he felt it was the one thing he could do better than she could. I draw great pictures and she doesn't.

4. What is the problem with this paragraph? _____

5. Which sentences need to be rewritten to make the point of view third-person

   omniscient throughout? _____

6. Rewrite those sentences. _____

   _____

In your Learning Log, write three sentences, each from a different point of view. Label which point of view each sentence represents.

Harcourt Brace School Publishers

Name _____

Read the following paragraph using context clues to determine the meaning of each underlined word. Then complete each sentence below by choosing the correct definition and writing it in the space provided.

Do you know how to keep <u>time</u> to music? It's not that hard. All you have to do is <u>stand</u> and clap your hands to the beat. Whenever I hear music, my body automatically <u>sways</u> with the music. What a <u>shock</u> it was when I learned that not everyone can feel the <u>rhythm</u> of music!

1. *Time* means _____
   a. the rate of movement in music
   b. a definite or appointed moment, hour, day, or period

2. *Stand* means _____
   a. a small table on which things may be placed
   b. to be in, or to place in, an upright position

3. *Sways* means _____
   a. causes to think in a certain way
   b. moves from side to side

4. *Shock* means _____
   a. tangle of hair
   b. sudden upset of mind or feelings

5. *Rhythm* means _____
   a. repetition, as of a beat, in a regular way
   b. an arrangement of line lengths and stresses in poetry

Name _____

Read the boldfaced words and their definitions in the box below. Then read each statement that follows and indicate whether or not you agree with it by putting a check mark by the appropriate answer. Write a sentence explaining why you agree or disagree.

professional:	someone who performs an art, sport, or skill for money
ensemble:	a group, such as actors or musicians, that performs together
intonation:	the pattern of rising and falling pitch
tempo:	the relative speed at which a musical piece is played
scales:	in music, a series of tones going up or down in order

1. If a person wants to play music, it is better to be a **professional** than just to play for fun. ☐ I agree ☐ I disagree

   The reason I think so is that _____.

2. A small musical **ensemble** is better than a big one. ☐ I agree ☐ I disagree

   The reason I think so is that _____.

3. **Intonation** doesn't really matter much in music. ☐ I agree ☐ I disagree

   The reason I think so is that _____.

4. A song with a slow **tempo** is boring. ☐ I agree ☐ I disagree

   The reason I think so is that _____.

5. Practicing **scales** is a waste of time for an advanced musician. ☐ I agree ☐ I disagree

   The reason I think so is that _____.

TRY THIS! Word Play

For each vocabulary word, make a list of all the shorter words you can make with the letters in that word. For example, here are just a few of the words you could make from the letters in *professional: profession, less, for, fan,* and *lion.* How many more can you think of? Have a contest with a partner to see who can find the most words.

Name _____

A. Look at the statements related to "A Very Young Musician." Use what you learned from the selection to decide if each statement is true or false.

Anticipation Guide	
Statement	**True or False?**
1. You can learn about music on a computer.	_____
2. A trumpet is easy to play while marching.	_____
3. It is the conductor's job to help a musical group perform together at the right speed.	_____
4. All woodwind instruments are made of wood.	_____
5. One of the oldest instruments is the flute.	_____
6. The French horn is an easy instrument to play.	_____

B. What qualities do you think are necessary to be a musician?

_____

_____

_____

_____

_____

_____

Name _____

A. Look at the pictures. Then finish the sentences by adding an action or linking verb to each.

Uncle Sean _____ Bea the gift.

She _____ the box open.

Her present _____ a shiny trumpet!

Bea _____ with a good music teacher.

She _____ every day.

She _____ her trumpet almost everywhere.

Before long, Bea _____ some other musicians.

They _____ a music group.

Their group _____ popular all over town.

B. Write two sentences about what Bea's music group did. Circle the verb in each sentence.

_____

_____

_____

_____

Tell a partner what you would say and do if you received a musical instrument as a gift. Use both action and linking verbs in your sentences.

Name _____

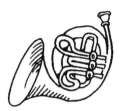

A. Imagine that a young musician talked to a magazine reporter and that you have to correct the interview. Find and circle the eight misspelled words. Then write the words correctly on the lines provided.

relax	invited	remind	review
unknown	interview	rehearse	recital

Reporter: Thank you for agreeing to let me intreview you. I understand that you have been envited to perform with the Chicago Symphony Orchestra. How do you feel about that?

Musician: It's such an honor for an onknown musician like myself to play with a famous orchestra! I'm a little scared, though, about how the audience will react to me and about the ruview of the concert.

Reporter: How will you prepare for the concert?

Musician: I practice every day for many hours. In addition to my regular practice, I will rahearse with the orchestra every day for a week.

Reporter: When did you first begin performing?

Musician: I performed in my first ricital when I was eight. I will never forget the feeling I had when I saw the audience. I was scared and nervous. I had to rimind myself that it was important for me to just rilax and play.

Reporter: Thank you, and good luck with the concert.

1. _____   4. _____   7. _____

2. _____   5. _____   8. _____

3. _____   6. _____

B. Add the correct prefix to complete each word from the box. Write the word on the line provided.

return	uncover	invented	uneasy
include	interrupt	unpleasant	intermediate

1. ____ cover _____   5. ____ clude _____

2. ____ easy _____   6. ____ turn _____

3. ____ pleasant _____   7. ____ rupt _____

4. ____ vented _____   8. ____ mediate _____

SPELLING: PREFIXES un-, re-, in-, AND inter-

Name _____

A. Each of the following scrolls contains specialized vocabulary words
used by a certain group of people. Read the words on each scroll.
Then, at the bottom of the scroll, identify the group of people who use
the words.

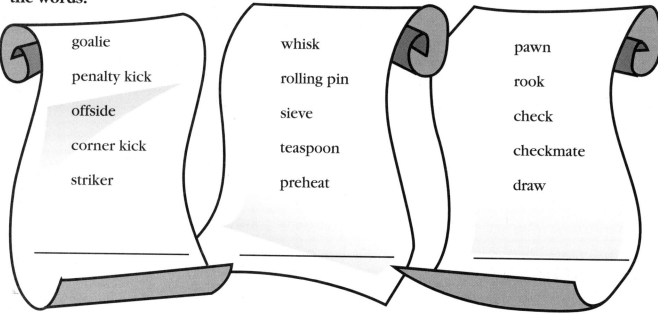

goalie

penalty kick

offside

corner kick

striker

_____

whisk

rolling pin

sieve

teaspoon

preheat

_____

pawn

rook

check

checkmate

draw

_____

B. Use the blank scrolls below to list specialized vocabularies used by
two different groups of people. Then read the words on your scrolls to
a partner to see whether he or she can identify groups of people who
use the words.

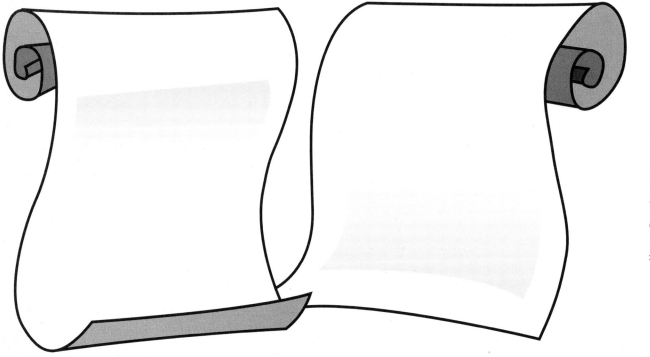

Harcourt Brace School Publishers

Name _____

A. Look at the Dewey Decimal System chart. Then answer the questions below.

Dewey Decimal System

000–099 General Reference Books
100–199 Philosophy
200–299 Religion
300–399 Social Sciences
400–499 Language
500–599 Pure Sciences
600–699 Technology
700–799 Arts and Recreation
800–899 Literature
900–999 General Geography and History

1. After meeting Wynton Marsalis, Josh wants to find out about other jazz trumpet players. In which section would he find information about them? _____

2. Josh is interested in playing duets with his computer. He needs software to help, but he also needs information about computers. In which section should he look? _____

3. Josh is looking for some poems that he can set to music. In which section will poetry be found? _____

4. Josh is in the chorus. They are learning songs in English, French, and German. He needs help with some German pronunciations. Where should he look? _____

5. Josh wants to read some adventure stories and mystery novels. Does he need to use the Dewey Decimal System? _____

6. How would he find fiction books?

_____

_____

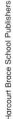

GO ON

B. Look at the Library of Congress System chart. Then answer the questions below.

Library of Congress System

A	General Works
B	Philosophy and Religion
C-D-E-F	History
H	Social Sciences
Q	Science
M	Music
N	Fine Arts
P	Language and Literature
T	Technology
Z	Libraries

1. Josh wants to do a report on the science of musical sounds. In what sections will he find the books he needs?

_____

2. The call number for the book Josh is looking for is C128. What type of book is he looking for?

_____

3. If Josh wanted to find information on China's past, where would he look?

_____

C. Answer the questions below, using both the Dewey Decimal System and the Library of Congress System charts.

1. The call number of a book Josh wants is 762.21. Which classification system does his library use?

_____

Under what subject is the book classified?

_____

2. Josh has to go to a different library. The call number of a book he wants is T112. Which classification system does this library use?

_____

Under which category is this book classified?

_____

Suppose you had to teach second graders how to use the library systems. In your Learning Log, write the steps you would tell these younger children to follow.

Name _____

Look at the following graphs. Then complete the chart below to compare and contrast the graphs.

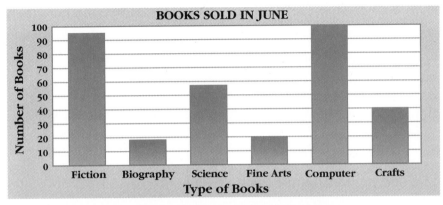

BOOKS SOLD IN JUNE

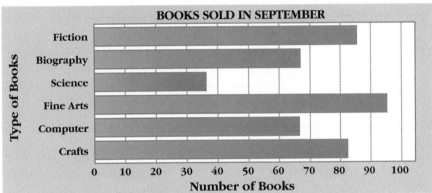

BOOKS SOLD IN SEPTEMBER

Ways in Which the Graphs Are the Same	Ways in Which the Graphs Are Different

Look around your classroom. Find two objects that you can compare and contrast. Describe the objects to a partner, focusing on the similarities and differences. Ask your partner to guess both objects. Then switch roles and guess your partner's objects.

Read each paragraph below and determine the point of view. Then answer the questions that follow.

Elisa was enjoying her vacation tour of New York City with her family. Their first stop was the Empire State Building. Elisa loved seeing the skyscrapers. Tim, her brother, especially liked Ellis Island. "I wonder," he thought, "what it must have been like to arrive on this island as an immigrant."

1. Which point of view is used in this paragraph? Circle your answer.

     first person   third person limited   third-person omniscient

2. What helped you identify the point of view?

   _____

   _____

   _____

Before we ever left on our vacation, I knew I wanted to visit the island of Alcatraz. I had read and heard about Alcatraz all my life. When we arrived in San Francisco and took the boat to the island, my family's reaction was disappointing. Both Elisa and Tim were bored, and even my husband was not very excited. "Oh, well," I thought, "we can't all be expected to like the same things."

3. Which point of view is used in this paragraph? Circle your answer.

     first person   third-person limited   third-person omniscient

4. What clues helped you identify the point of view?

   _____

   _____

   _____

Describe an event that took place in the classroom, using two different points of view.

Harcourt Brace School Publishers

Name _____

Read the boldfaced words and their definitions in the box below. Then read the clusters of words that follow and decide which vocabulary word is most closely related to the words or phrases in the cluster. Write that vocabulary word in the center of the cluster.

dreadful:	shocking; awful
peculiar:	strange
symphony:	a piece of music written to be played by an orchestra
inquiries:	questions
uproar:	a disturbance or noisy confusion
appreciated:	understood and valued
eccentricities:	behaviors that are odd

appalling   offensive

terrible   hideous

research   investigation

riot   furor

quiz   examination

clamor   hubbub

unusual   bizarre

composer   woodwinds

extraordinary   exceptional

conductor   score

prized   treasured

oddities   strangeness

applauded   admired

unusual habits   offbeat qualities

TRY THIS! Word Play

In a small group, tell a story using the vocabulary words. Each group sits in a circle and one person makes up the first sentence. Then the second person makes up the second sentence, and so on. As you take turns, write the story down so you can share it with another group.

Name _____

A. Complete the story map about "Beethoven Lives Upstairs."

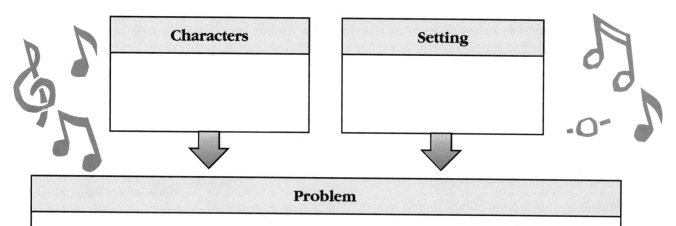

Characters	Setting

Problem

Important Events

Resolution

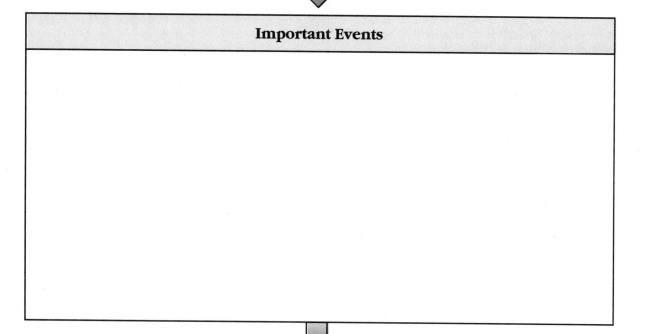

B. Why do you think the author wrote this story?

_____

_____

Harcourt Brace School Publishers

Name _____

Read each question. Draw one line under the helping verb and two lines under the main verb. (Remember that in most questions the helping verb and the main verb are separated by one or more other words.) Then use a helping verb and a main verb to write an answer to the question.

1. Have you ever played the piano?

   _____

2. Are you taking music lessons?

   _____

3. Have you ever attended a live concert?

   _____

4. What kind of music are you studying?

   _____

5. Can you introduce me to any musicians?

   _____

6. What are you listening to right now?

   _____

7. What should you do later today?

   _____

8. What will you do next week?

   _____

What musician would you most like to interview? On a separate sheet of paper, write five interview questions you would ask that performer or composer.

Name _____

A. Help Christoph finish a letter to his uncle. Add the missing *dis-* or *de-* prefix to each incomplete word. Write the word on the line provided.

decided   details   design   develop   delight
describe   defense   disability   disturbed
disadvantage   dissatisfied
disappointed

Dear Uncle,

I am very _____appointed now that Beethoven has moved. I felt we were beginning to _____velop a friendship. I had _____cided that he was very special and talented—a genius. Now I am _____satisfied with my other friends. Although he disliked being _____turbed, he often took _____light in my visits. They gave him a chance to _____scribe his work. He even told me the smallest _____tails about how he was planning the Ninth Symphony. When I questioned his _____sign for the work, he spoke strongly in _____fense of his ideas. Now, after hearing a performance of the Ninth Symphony, I believe he knew exactly what he was doing! Many people would have found a hearing _____ability a major _____advantage for a composer, but not the great Beethoven.

Your Nephew,

Christoph

1. _____   5. _____   9. _____

2. _____   6. _____   10. _____

3. _____   7. _____   11. _____

4. _____   8. _____   12. _____

B. For each word, decide which prefix is needed to form a word from the box. Write the word on the line provided.

discount
degree
demand
deduct

1. ___ gree   _____   3. ___ count   _____

2. ___ duct   _____   4. ___ mand   _____

Harcourt Brace School Publishers

Name _____

Read the music-related words in the box and the riddles below. Then, in the space provided, write the word that answers each riddle.

conductor	piano	composer	violin
musicians	rehearsal	soprano	singers

1. We practice playing by day and by night.
   Our rehearsal load is heavy, not light.

   _____

2. We make music with only our voices.
   Our sounds are really some of the choicest.

   _____

3. Practice, practice is what I say.
   When you come to me, you'll play, play, play.

   _____

4. Letters and words are not what I do.
   Writing notes is what I pursue.

   _____

5. I can play music fast or slow.
   You can play me by drawing a bow.

   _____

6. I have 88 keys of black and white.
   I can be either grand or upright.

   _____

7. With my baton I lead the band.
   When it follows, the sound is grand.

   _____

8. I perform what a composer wrote.
   I can always reach the highest note.

   _____

Choose one music word from the list or from the story. On a separate piece of paper, write each letter vertically. Then write a word for each letter that has to do with music. Your words might look like this:

M usician
U nison
S ounds
I nstruments
C oncert

EXTENDING VOCABULARY: MUSIC WORDS **121**

A. Look at the types of slanted or biased writing listed in the box. Then read the advertisements and answer the questions.

> loaded words   name-calling   glittering generalities

BEETHOVEN'S FIFTH
Be sure to buy a ticket to the greatest concert on Earth.
You will hear music that is just out of this world.
Only a music hater would miss it.

1. What techniques does this ad use to persuade people to attend the concert?

_____

_____

2. What glittering generalities are used in the ad? _____

_____

3. Who is called a name in the ad? _____

_____

Name _____

SHAMPOO FOR YOU

Don't be a dandruff-head any longer!
Try the best shampoo both east and west of the Mississippi.

100% GUARANTEED TO MAKE YOUR HAIR BEHAVE.
BUY **SHAMPOO FOR YOU**.

4. What techniques does this ad use to persuade people to buy the shampoo?

_____

5. What is the name people are called?

_____

6. What loaded words are used in the ad?

_____

B. Write your own ad to sell a product or an event. Use two slanted or biased writing techniques.

_____

_____

_____

_____

_____

_____

_____

TRY THIS!
Learning Log

Identifying slanted or biased writing is helpful when reading ads, newspaper headlines, and editorials. In your Learning Log, write how you can tell when writing is slanted or biased.

Look at the words and their meanings in the chart. Then read each sentence below and select the appropriate meaning for the underlined word. Write it in the space provided.

Word	Meanings
sail	a. cloth that catches wind to move a boat b. to move in a boat
craft	a. a skill or an occupation b. a ship, boat, or aircraft
mission	a. something a person sets out to do b. a religious outpost
passed	a. moved past or went by b. voted in favor of, approved
named	a. appointed to a job or an office b. gave a name to
reached	a. stretched one's hand or arm out b. arrived at or came to
completed	a. made whole with nothing missing b. ended or finished

1. Ferdinand Magellan was the first explorer to <u>sail</u> around the world.

   In this sentence, *sail* means _____.

2. His <u>craft</u> had to travel from Spain across the Atlantic to South America.

   In this sentence, *craft* means _____.

3. From there his <u>mission</u> was to sail along the eastern shore until he reached the southernmost tip.

   In this sentence, *mission* means _____.

4. Magellan <u>passed</u> through a strait now named for him and found a great ocean.

   In this sentence, *passed* means _____.

5. He <u>named</u> this great ocean the Pacific Ocean, which means "peaceful ocean."

   In this sentence, *named* means _____.

6. Magellan continued sailing across the Pacific Ocean and <u>reached</u> the Philippine Islands.

   In this sentence, *reached* means _____.

7. After Magellan's death, his crew sailed on and <u>completed</u> the historic voyage around the world.

   In this sentence, *completed* means _____.

Name _____

Read each sentence, using context clues to determine the meaning of the boldfaced words. Then, from the group of words that follow, circle the word that means the same as the boldfaced word.

1. The **cooperative** got better deals on groceries because all the members put their money together to buy in bulk.

   association   playground   butcher   pharmacy

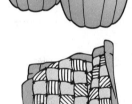

2. Thelma got a great price on **poultry** at the chicken ranch.

   fish   beef   fowl   feathers

3. After the **harvest,** the price of pumpkins came down because there were so many available.

   planting   weeding   winter   crop gathering

4. Joseph got a better deal on 100 percent natural fabric than he could get on **synthetic** fabric.

   silk   artificially produced   linen   paper

5. Everyone can enjoy the play equipment in the park because it is for **communal** use.

   private   public   summer   children's

6. The people were trying to **perpetuate** a small-town way of life so that their children would be able to enjoy it, too.

   end   abolish   appreciate   continue

TRY THIS!
Writing

Imagine that you are a farmer. On a separate piece of paper, write a diary entry for a typical day on the farm using at least four of the vocabulary words. Share your entry with a partner.

Harcourt Brace School Publishers

A. Complete the K-W-L chart about "The American Family Farm."

K	W	L
What I Know	**What I Want to Know**	**What I Learned**

B. What did you learn from this story that you could apply to your everyday life?

_____

_____

_____

_____

_____

Harcourt Brace School Publishers

Name _____

Read each sentence, and underline the verb. Then write *present*, *past*, or *future* to identify the tense of the verb.

1. We work hard!

   _____

2. This project takes a long

   time. _____

3. We started this project two days

   ago. _____

4. With luck, we will finish

   tomorrow. _____

5. We dried these beans in the sun.

   _____

6. I sort the beans.

   _____

7. Later we will add a label to each

   bag. _____

8. Our customers will use these beans in soups and stews.

   _____

9. Last year we sold more than a ton of beans.

   _____

10. Our business grows every

    year. _____

11. We will put the beans into

    bags. _____

TRY THIS! Writing

On a separate sheet of paper, write three sentences of your own, using verbs in the future tense. Challenge a partner to rewrite your sentences, using the same verbs in the past tense.

Name _____

A. The new president of the co-op is talking to old and new members about the group's purpose. Circle the word in parentheses that is spelled correctly. Write the correct spellings on the lines provided.

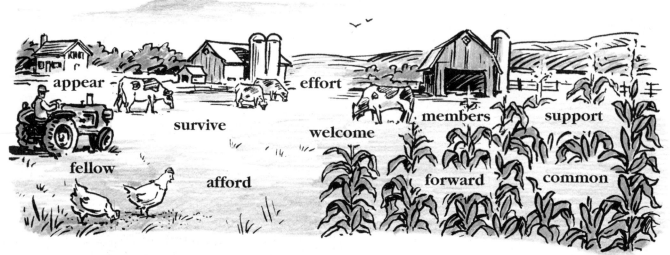

appear   effort   members   support

survive   welcome

fellow   afford   forward   common

I (wellcome, welcome) old and new (membrs, members) alike to today's meeting of our co-op. We have (commen, common) goals and needs. Together we can move our farms (forward, forwurd) by providing each other with moral as well as physical (suport, support). None of us can (aford, afford) to do without the others. As a group, we will (appear, eppear) stronger to those who want to force or buy us out. Through a joint (effert, effort), we will be able to (survive, surrvive) whatever obstacles come our way. My friends and (fellow, felow) members, I am hopeful that we will have many years together.

1. _____   5. _____   9. _____

2. _____   6. _____   10. _____

3. _____   7. _____

4. _____   8. _____

B. Unscramble each group of letters to form a word from the box. Write the word on the line provided.

window
circus
tennis
object
narrow
office

1. succir _____   4. dnowwi _____

2. fcefio _____   5. sinten _____

3. ronraw _____   6. jtebco _____

Name _____

A. Read the following passage. Then fill in the chart below.

Have you ever visited a farm? Last year I spent a week feeding chickens, milking cows, and riding horses on a farm. Once I got past all the earthy smells, I discovered that I really liked animals. I had never spent much time around animals before, except perhaps dogs and birds.

One of the greatest and most exciting things about being on the farm was the sharing and working together. People on a farm learn from each other, and everyone pitches in to help. One night everyone went to a neighbor's farm for a square dance. I had thought square dancing was strictly for the movies. What fun it was! We danced, watched the stars, and finished the evening with a hayride.

Before I went to the farm, I thought farm life would be boring. I was wrong. It was great!

Main Idea

Detail	Detail	Detail

GO ON

Name _____

B. Look at the pictures below. Write a main idea sentence for each one.

Main Idea: _____

_____

Main Idea: _____

_____

Main Idea: _____

_____

Look through magazine or newspaper articles. In your Learning Log, explain how you would identify the main ideas and details of the articles.

Name _____

Read the boldfaced words and their definitions on the buggy. Create a word web for two of the vocabulary words, as shown in the example.

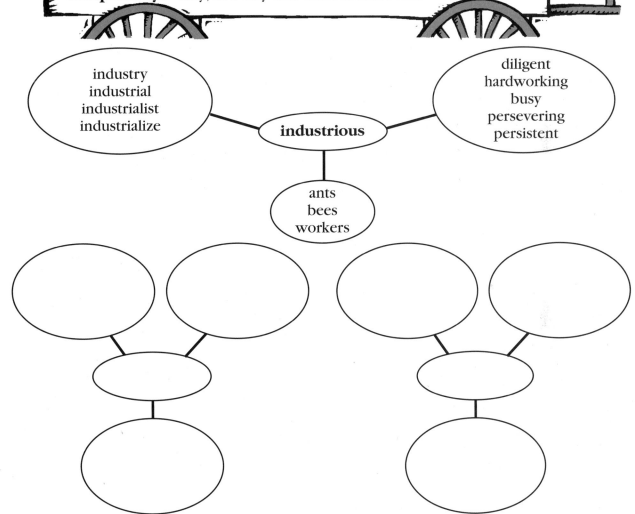

industrious:	hardworking and diligent
emphasizes:	stresses; points out for special notice
depriving:	keeping from having or enjoying
dialect:	a form of speech characteristic of a certain area or class, with its own words, idioms, and pronunciations
tolerate:	to put up with
competently:	ably; in a way that demonstrates skill

industry
industrial
industrialist
industrialize

industrious

diligent
hardworking
busy
persevering
persistent

ants
bees
workers

TRY THIS! Word Play

How many words can you find hidden within the vocabulary words? Have a contest with a partner to see who can find more words. The letters that spell your new words must be found in that order in the vocabulary word. For example, you'll find *pet, ten,* and *tent* in *competently*.

A. Summarize "Amish Home" by completing the Knowledge Chart.

Knowledge Chart	
Prior Knowledge About the Amish	**New Knowledge About the Amish**

B. What is the most important lesson you learned from this story?

_____

_____

_____

Harcourt Brace School Publishers

Name _____

A. Complete the following announcement. Read the past-tense verbs in parentheses. Then write the present-tense form of each verb on the line.

New Quilt Show

The Folk Treasures Quilt Show (opened) _____ today in City Hall.

The show (featured) _____ more than fifty quilts. Several Amish quilts

(highlighted) _____ the show. These quilts (displayed) _____

surprising bursts of color and clever needlework. The show also (included)

_____ quilts from the southern states. Beautiful decorations (marked)

_____ these quilts as special. Several quilts (reflected) _____ the

frontier style. One (mixed) _____ printed fabrics in blue, orange, and pink.

B. Leila went to the quilt show. Then she sent a postcard to her grandmother. Read the present-tense verbs in parentheses. Then complete her card by writing the past-tense form of the verb on the line.

Dear Gran,

Polly and I (visit) _____ a quilt show
today. I (admire) _____ the designs, and the
tiny stitches (amaze) _____ me! The quilt
on this card (reminds) _____ me of you.
Don't forget, you (promise) _____ to teach
me how to quilt!

Love,
Leila

Make your own postcard. Draw a picture on one side of the card. On the other side, write a message to a friend. Tell about a place you have visited or something interesting you have done. Use present-tense verbs and past-tense verbs.

Name _____

A. Imagine that you are visiting Amish country. Complete this postcard to a friend by adding the missing letter to each incomplete word. Write the word on the line provided.

merchant	improve	display	instead
purchase	increase	although	complex

Dear Erin,

A group of people called the Amish live in this part of Pennsylvania. In___tead of having modern conveniences such as cars, they use a horse and buggy. Alt___ough these people do not have a com___lex lifestyle, they do seem to have a very good life. After one day without television or radio, conversation within my family certainly did in___rease! The Amish dis___lay good sense when it comes to things they must pur___hase. Any mer___hant hoping to sell lots of material goods should not settle in Amish country. However, if anyone is of a mind to change or im___rove his or her lifestyle, this simple way may be the best.

Your friend,

Jessica

1. _____   4. _____   7. _____

2. _____   5. _____   8. _____

3. _____   6. _____

B. Fill in the missing letters to complete the words from the box. Then write each word on the line provided.

1. go that e __ __ __ a mile _____

2. apple o__ __ __ ard _____

3. representative in Co __ __ __ __ ess _____

4. fireworks e __ __ __ ode _____

5. o __ __ __ ich feathers _____

6. cats such as jaguar, leopard, and pa __ __ __ er _____

7. paint a po __ __ __ ait _____

8. travel no fa __ __ __ er than your own backyard _____

farther
explode
extra
orchard
ostrich
panther
Congress
portrait

Harcourt Brace School Publishers

Name _____

Look at each picture and the boldfaced foreign word below it. Determine the English meaning of each foreign word based on the picture. Write the meaning on the lines provided.

_____

_____

rumpaspringa (German)

hacienda (Spanish)

_____

_____

_____

_____

cul-de-sac (French)

ciao (Italian)

_____

_____

_____

_____

wihio (Cheyenne)

Work in a group. Each group member should write a foreign word—from another selection, from a dictionary, or from personal experience—on one side of an index card and its English definition on the back. Then lay the cards down with the foreign word facing up. Take turns guessing at the English meanings.

A. Read the meanings of the prefixes, suffixes, and word roots in the box. Then read the sentences below. Use context clues and structural analysis to determine the meaning of each boldface word. Underline the correct meaning.

re-	again	*de-*	reduce
un-	not	*-ity*	condition of being
-vis-	see	*-ous*	full of

1. Many Amish teenagers are very **studious.**
   a. not studying
   b. full of studying
   c. against studying

2. Someone who had visited the Amish 60 years ago would find them still **unchanged** by modern life.
   a. totally changed
   b. slightly changed
   c. not changed

3. Telephones and modern appliances are a **rarity** in Amish country.
   a. condition of being common
   b. condition of being rare
   c. condition of being popular

4. There is a **visible** difference between the Amish and their visitors.
   a. capable of being seen
   b. capable of being touched
   c. capable of being heard

5. By using horses instead of tractors on their farms, the Amish believe they can **decrease** their costs.
   a. make or become less
   b. make or become more
   c. keep the same

6. After living among the Amish for several days, some people might be happy to **return** to their modern conveniences.
   a. stay away from
   b. turn again
   c. try to find

Harcourt Brace School Publishers

Name _____

B. Match each word with its correct definition, using the prefixes, suffixes, and word roots in the box as clues. Write the letter of the definition on the line next to the word.

bio-	*life*
-graph-	*write*
pre-	*before*
en-	*into*
ex-	*out*
un-	*not*

_____ **1.** prearranged   **a.** outside

_____ **2.** biography   **b.** arranged in advance

_____ **3.** encourage   **c.** not like

_____ **4.** exterior   **d.** life story

_____ **5.** unlike   **e.** put hope into

C. Make a list of other words that contain the prefixes, suffixes, and root words from above.

bio- : _____

-graph- : _____

pre- : _____

en- : _____

ex- : _____

un- : _____

TRY THIS! Learning Log

In your Learning Log, list some prefixes, suffixes, and word roots along with their meanings. Then write phrases to serve as clues for words that have those prefixes, suffixes, and roots. Take turns with a partner. Ask your partner to figure out which word matches each clue. Do the same for your partner's clues.

Name _____

Read the following paragraph. Then fill in the main idea and details in the chart below.

Eating too much food can make a person gain unwanted weight. Eating moderate amounts of high-calorie foods can also make a person gain weight. Be careful not to eat just because you have nothing else to do. Also, be careful not to eat because you are worried or under stress. Those are two sure ways people can add unwanted pounds. Regular exercise and a balanced diet are the keys to good health. It's easy! People can maintain a healthful weight and keep off unwanted pounds simply by keeping these tips in mind.

Main Idea

Detail	Detail	Detail	Detail

On a separate sheet of paper, write a paragraph that has this main idea: *Some snacks are good for you.* Support this idea with at least three details.

Harcourt Brace School Publishers

Name _____

Read each sentence or group of sentences, using context clues to determine the meaning of the boldfaced word. Then, from the three definitions that follow, circle the one that most closely explains the boldfaced word, based on the clues in the sentence.

1. It was July, the second month of the four-month **monsoon** in India. As usual, it was very rainy.

   a wet season   a hot, humid season   a dry season

2. Even though it would be a great personal **sacrifice,** Khalil had agreed to baby-sit for the afternoon. It would mean not having time to play baseball with his friends.

   giving up of something   gaining a reward   forgetting something

3. Khalil's parents went to a party that **commemorated** the anniversary of their neighbors' wedding.

   honored the memory of   made fun of   changed the appearance of

4. Khalil taught his little sister about the importance of **conservation.** He reminded her not to leave the water running while she was brushing her teeth because it was wasteful.

   saving of resources   wasting of resources   giving away resources

5. When Khalil's parents got back, they spoke about their friends' plans for the **restoration** of some old furniture. They would sand it down, repaint it, and make it look like new.

   bringing something back to look new   destroying something

   throwing something away

TRY THIS! Word Play

Play a game of opposites with a partner. For some of the vocabulary words, write on an index card a word or expression that means the opposite. Take turns with a partner choosing cards and identifying the vocabulary word that has the opposite meaning.

Name _____

A. Summarize "The People Who Hugged the Trees" by completing the story map.

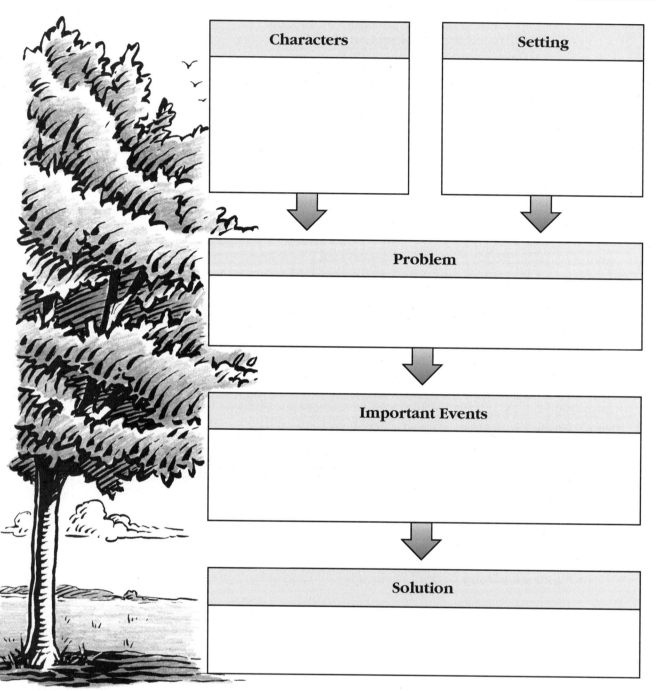

Characters	Setting

Problem

Important Events

Solution

B. Is there anything you would be willing to take a risk for? Describe it.

_____

_____

_____

Harcourt Brace School Publishers

Name _____

Complete the sentences on this bulletin board. Read the present-tense verb below the line. Then write the past-tense form of the verb on the line.

Congratulations to everyone in Greenville!

We _____ problems beginning to develop in our environment—and we
    see

_____ something about those problems. We _____ the
    do   begin

Greenville Recycles program ten years ago. This week, every Greenville resident

_____ at least one aluminum can or one old newspaper to our recycling
   brings

center. Each of those recycled items _____ a difference. Some people have
                                        makes

taken extra steps. Mr. Shaw's fifth graders _____ to local factories, asking
                                     write

them to help keep our air and water clean. A group of middle-school students invited

Senator Dirks to visit Greenville, and she _____ here. In her speech that
                                     comes

day, the senator _____ she will continue to support efforts to keep our
         says

environment clean. The Kindergarten Chorus _____ "Keep Us Green" at
                                      sings

the last Greenville City Council meeting.

RECYCLE

TRY THIS! Writing

Design your own bulletin board to congratulate people on a job well done. Include both pictures and sentences on your bulletin board. Use past-tense verb forms in your sentences.

Name _____

A. These environmental slogans might make their point better if they
were spelled correctly. Find and circle the misspelled words. Then
write each word correctly on the line provided.

robin	travel	began	vacant	finish	minutes	desert

Avoid Living in a Dezert; Save a Tree

Clean Up a Vakant Lot; Clean Up the Earth

1. _____

2. _____

It Takes Only Minnutes to Make a Mess That
Can Last for Years

Travle by Foot, Not by Car

3. _____

4. _____

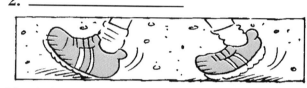

Let's Not Finsih What Others Beggan

Where Will the Ropin Live When There Are
No Trees?

5. _____

6. _____

7. _____

B. Complete these words from the box by filling in the missing vowel-
consonant-vowel letter group. Then write the word on the line provided.

even	peanut	moment	chosen	private	item	solid	balance	basin

1. m _ _ _ nt   _____

2. s _ _ _ d   _____

3. ch _ _ _ n   _____

4. _ _ _ m   _____

5. pe _ _ _ t   _____

6. b _ _ _ nce   _____

7. b _ _ _ n   _____

8. _ _ _ n   _____

9. pr _ _ _ te   _____

Name _____

Read the following information about environmental problems. Then answer the questions.

RECYCLING—YES OR NO

We've seen all those bins for newspapers and for plastic and other types of containers. Many people sort their waste using these bins. Some people, however, don't seem to care. If you recycle paper, you are doing more than saving trees. You are also saving energy that is used to cut down trees to make them into paper. You are also keeping waste dumps from filling up. In one year with recycling, 5 million trees can be saved. Isn't putting your old newspapers in a bin worth the effort?

What important information did you learn from this source?

_____

_____

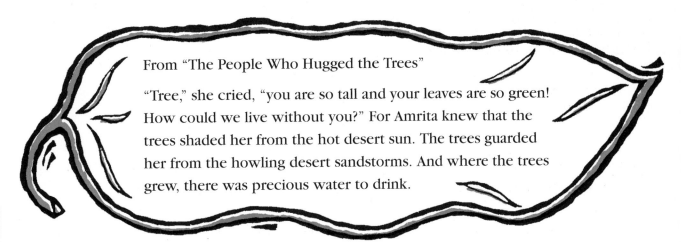

From "The People Who Hugged the Trees"

"Tree," she cried, "you are so tall and your leaves are so green! How could we live without you?" For Amrita knew that the trees shaded her from the hot desert sun. The trees guarded her from the howling desert sandstorms. And where the trees grew, there was precious water to drink.

Why would Amrita find it difficult to live without the trees?

_____

_____

Name _____

Causes of Water Pollution

Type of Substance	What It Is Used for	Harmful Effects
Pesticide	sprayed on plants to kill insects	Rain washes pesticides off plants and into bodies of water. Pesticides can harm other living things besides insect pests.
Fertilizer	added to soil to help plants grow	Excess fertilizer stays in the soil. When it rains, the fertilizer can be washed into a river or lake and pollute the water.
Detergent	used for cleaning	Chemicals in detergents get into the drains of homes and can get into lakes, rivers, and streams.

Write a main idea you learned from this chart.

_____

_____

Based on all the sources you have read, write a conclusion that combines the information.

_____

_____

In your Learning Log, describe how you would synthesize information if you were writing a report on the environment or another topic in science.

Name _____

Read the paragraphs. Then answer the questions that follow.

Maria Martinez was a Pueblo Indian from New Mexico who lived from 1887 to 1980. At a young age she learned to make pots as her ancestors had done. Her pots were not just ordinary pots. In fact, they were so special that museums all over the world wanted them.

Maria Martinez's pots were made of clay that she dug up from the ground near her home. Her hands were the tools she used to shape the clay. Then she used stones to rub the pots. Often she painted designs on them. Then she baked them in a hot oven.

Maria passed her pot-making skills on to members of her family, who now continue to make the shiny black pots. They continue to do what their ancestors did more than 700 years ago.

1. What is the unstated main idea of the first paragraph?

_____

_____

2. What details helped you identify the main idea?

_____

_____

3. What is the unstated main idea of the second paragraph?

_____

_____

4. What details support this main idea?

_____

_____

5. What is the unstated main idea of the last paragraph?

_____

_____

Harcourt Brace School Publishers

TRY THIS!
Talking Tip

Think about something interesting that happened to you last week. Tell your class what happened. Include details that will help your audience understand what happened and help them identify a main idea.

Name _____

A. Look at the root words and their meanings in the box. Then complete each sentence with a word that contains the root shown in parentheses.

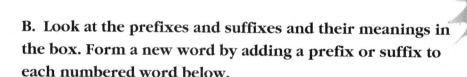

astro- star	**tele-** far away
vis- see	

1. A person who travels into space is an _____ (*astro-*)

2. Galileo used a _____ to look at distant stars. (*tele-*)

3. He was able to see things that were not _____ to the naked eye. (*vis-*)

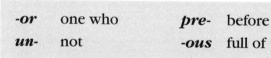

B. Look at the prefixes and suffixes and their meanings in the box. Form a new word by adding a prefix or suffix to each numbered word below.

-or one who	**pre-** before
un- not	**-ous** full of
mis- incorrectly	

1. lock

   New word: _____

2. invent

   New word: _____

3. heat

   New word: _____

4. danger

   New word: _____

5. understood

   New word: _____

Name _____

Read the boldfaced words and their definitions. Then complete the story with the correct boldfaced words.

inhabit:	to occupy; to live in
distribution:	the act of dividing and dealing out in shares
nutrients:	foods; things that give nourishment
desolate:	lacking people; deserted
vegetation:	plant life
irrigation:	the act of supplying water to land by using pipes, ditches, or canals
ecosystems:	communities of living things
impact:	the force or influence of one thing on another

The settlers rode through the dry and _____

land, but they knew they could never _____

such a place. They continued traveling until they found an area

where the _____ was a little thicker and

included trees with edible fruit. They knew that

_____ of crops would not be a problem because

rainfall was frequent and a river crossed the land.

After everyone had staked a claim, the

_____ of deeds for the land took place. The

settlers added _____ to the soil to make it

richer and more likely to produce new crops. They were

concerned about their _____ on the land, so

they tried to take good care of it. But no matter how careful they

were, they disturbed several delicate _____ as

the population grew and needed more space.

On a separate piece of paper, draw a picture clue for each vocabulary word. Work with a partner. Have your partner try to guess each word using your clue.

A. Complete the SQ3R chart to summarize "The Third Planet."

Survey	Question	Review

B. What could you say about planet Earth after reading this selection?

_____

_____

_____

_____

Harcourt Brace School Publishers

Name _____

A. Read the following paragraph, and underline the future-tense verbs you find.

     People have already spent long periods of time in space. The first human orbited the Earth in 1961. Now, space shuttles and space stations are regular parts of our space exploration programs. We will begin new programs in the near future. New spacecraft will take off, and more people will spend time in space. Someday, people will plan colonies in open space and on other planets. Perhaps you will volunteer for one of these new space programs!

B. Complete each sentence by adding a future-tense verb.

1. Space explorers _____ more facts about the planets in our solar system.

2. Each space flight _____ our understanding.

3. Maybe someday people _____ their whole lives in space.

4. Talented students from many parts of the world _____ astronaut-training programs.

5. Knowledge gained from space programs _____ the lives of people here on Earth.

TRY THIS!
Talking Tip

Tell a partner what you think might happen with space exploration during your lifetime. Use some verbs in the future tense.

**A. Fix this newspaper clipping by correcting the underlined words.
Then write the correct spelling on the line provided.**

We have much to learn about the Earth. <u>Priur</u> studies done years ago seemed to pay more attention to other planets than to Earth. Without knowledge of our home planet, we could not <u>reakt</u> to global challenges, such as our <u>gient</u> need for <u>fuul</u>. <u>Scyence</u> can now use satellites to gather information about our planet. What a great <u>triomph</u> it will be when we have discovered all that Earth has to tell!

prior	react	science
giant	triumph	fuel

1. _____

2. _____

3. _____

4. _____

5. _____

6. _____

**B. Unscramble each group of letters to form a word from the box.
Write the word on the line provided.**

liar	quiet	cruel	riot	diet	ruin
poem	poet	lion	create		

1. uietq _____

2. rlia _____

3. ulecr _____

4. tori _____

5. nuri _____

6. tdei _____

7. mpeo _____

8. nloi _____

9. tpeo _____

10. cetrae _____

Name _____

Find your way from Mercury to Pluto. Use the acronyms and abbreviations in the spaceship with the clues below to fill in each blank.

1. _____   2. _____   3. _____

4. _____   5. _____   6. _____

7. _____   8. _____   9. _____

Clue # 1: If you wanted to travel to Mercury, you'd probably go to the National Aeronautics and Space Administration. _____

Clue # 2: You won't be able to play this on Venus. It is an abbreviation for a compact disc. _____

Clue # 3: On Earth your computer is only as powerful as your random-access memory. _____

Clue # 4: If there's any life on Mars, maybe it can be found using radio detecting and ranging. _____

Clue # 5: December 31 is nowhere near the end of the year on Jupiter. _____

Clue # 6: There's no water on Saturn, so there's no sound navigation ranging. _____

Clue # 7: Artificial intelligence is the only kind you will find on Uranus. _____

Clue # 8: When it's Wednesday on Earth, it's probably not on Neptune. _____

Clue # 9: Light amplification by stimulated emission of radiation would give Pluto more light. _____

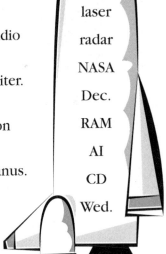

sonar
laser
radar
NASA
Dec.
RAM
AI
CD
Wed.

Play with a partner. Each of you writes down five acronyms or abbreviations and the word or words they stand for. Then, take turns saying an acronym or abbreviation aloud while your partner guesses what it stands for.

Name _____

A. Read the following paragraphs. Then complete the outline below.

There is no air on the moon. Because of this, the moon has almost no atmosphere at all. There is absolutely no oxygen on the moon to breathe.

The moon's surface has mountains, highlands, and flat areas. Craters formed long ago when large rocks hit the moon. Many of these craters then filled with lava during volcanic eruptions.

The Moon

I. Air on the Moon

    A. _____

    B. _____

II. The Moon's Surface

    A. _____

    B. _____

        1. _____

        2. _____

Harcourt Brace School Publishers

Name _____

B. Read the following paragraphs. Then fill in the cards below according to the directions.

You may not feel it, but you are moving every day, all day. Earth makes a trip around the sun every year. This trip is called a revolution. It takes Earth 365 1/4 days to revolve around the sun. That's why our year is 365 1/4 days long. All the planets revolve around the sun, but each planet takes a different time to finish one trip. The closer a planet is to the sun, the less time it takes to complete its revolution. It takes Mercury only 88 days. Because Pluto is farthest away from the sun, it has the greatest distance to travel. It takes Pluto 248 1/2 years to complete one revolution.

Earth and the other planets also spin, or rotate, at the same time that they revolve. It takes one day—24 hours—for Earth to complete one spin. On Jupiter, it takes only 10 hours to complete a spin. On Venus, a spin, or rotation, takes 243 days.

Record the main idea and supporting details from the first paragraph on this card.

On this card, record the main idea and supporting details from the second paragraph.

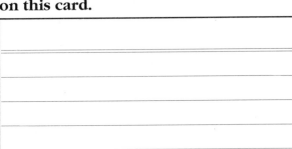

Now use the note cards to complete the outline.

How Planets Move

I. _____

   A. _____

   B. _____

II. _____

   A. _____

   B. _____

TRY THIS! Learning Log

Taking concise notes and learning how to make an outline of what you read are important study skills. In your Learning Log, explain what things should be included in an outline.

Name _____

Look at the chart and then read each sentence below. In the space provided, write the word that contains a root, a prefix, or a suffix from the chart. Then circle the root, prefix, or suffix.

-mete-	measure	*tri-*	three	*-graph-*	write
-struct-	build	*-tract-*	pull	*-cent-*	hundred
-sect-	divide	*dec-*	ten	*-form-*	shape

1. We learned how to subtract in first grade. _____

2. You answered 90 percent of the questions correctly. _____

3. The thermometer on the wall read 75 degrees. _____

4. Where do those two roads intersect? _____

5. Her sister was born a decade before her. _____

6. What is the formula for this math problem? _____

7. A green centipede crawled across the patio floor. _____

8. My little sister likes to draw triangles. _____

9. The data would be easier to understand if we used a graphic

    aid. _____

10. I didn't understand the instructions for the last question.

    _____

Name _____

Read the boldfaced words and their definitions in the box. What related words do you think of when you read each vocabulary word? Write your ideas in the word webs. Two words have been added as examples for you.

founded:	set up; established (as a school, a company, a city)
adobe:	a brick that is made of sun-dried clay and straw
mesas:	hills or small plateaus with steep sides and a flat top
cultivated:	planted and cared for
accomplishment:	the act of completing or achieving something

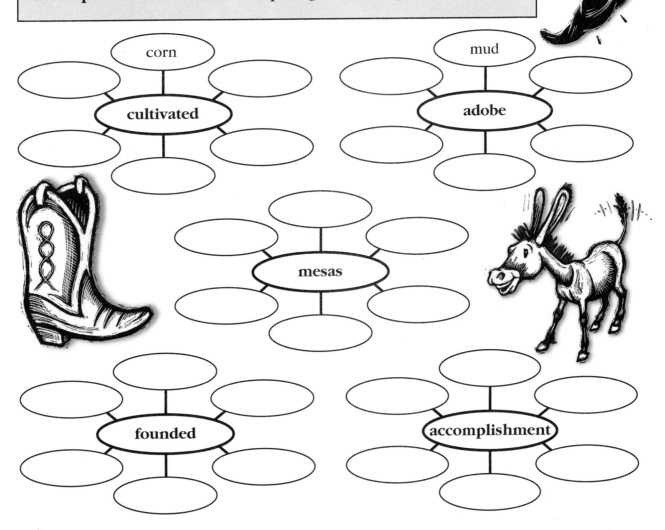

corn

cultivated

mud

adobe

mesas

founded

accomplishment

TRY THIS! Word Play

Work with a partner. Write each vocabulary word on a separate index card. On other index cards, write one related word for each vocabulary word. Lay all cards face down in random order. Try to find a matching pair by turning two cards over. If they match, keep the pair and take another turn. If they don't match, turn them face down again. The play then passes to your partner.

Name _____

**A. Summarize "Spanish Pioneers of the Southwest" by completing
the K-W-L chart.**

K	W	L
What I Know	**What I Want to Know**	**What I Learned**

**B. What do you think you would have learned if you had spent time
with the Spanish pioneers of the Southwest?**

_____

_____

_____

_____

Name _____

Early Pueblo peoples built large cliff dwellings in an area now called Mesa Verde. Imagine that you and others visited Mesa Verde not long ago. Read each question, and write a one-sentence answer. Use an adverb from the box in each of your answers.

carefully
nearby
recently
soon
thoroughly
really

1. When did you visit Mesa Verde?

_____

2. How did you explore the ruins?

_____

3. How do the archaeologists examine the Mesa Verde artifacts?

_____

4. Where did you stay during your visit?

_____

5. To what extent were the cliff dwellings awesome?

_____

6. When would you like to return to Mesa Verde?

_____

TRY THIS!
Talking Tip

Tell a partner about another interesting place you have visited or read about. Use at least two adverbs.

A. Find and circle the eight misspelled words in the description of Miguel's home. Then write the words correctly on the lines below.

fireplace   backyard   background   farmland
doorway   everybody   outdoors   rattlesnake

The land beyond the hacienda is like a giant back yard park. It is wide and open and full of nature's creatures, even the occasional rattle snake. It is a fitting back ground to the fort. Every body on the hacienda works to make the things they need to live. When Miguel returns from the farm land, his mama is standing in the door way of the fortress. She cooks meals in the fire place. After spending the day out doors, everyone enjoys their warm home.

1. _____   4. _____   7. _____

2. _____   5. _____   8. _____

3. _____   6. _____

B. Compound words are made up of two or more small words. The first part of each compound word below is given. Use the clue to figure out the second part. Write the complete word on the line provided.

1. earth + a word that rhymes with *shake*   _____

2. Thanks + a word that rhymes with *living*   _____

3. brand + the opposite of *old*   _____

4. seventy + the number after *four*   _____

5. up + a word that means   _____
   "something you can climb"

6. life + a word that rhymes with *hard*   _____

7. flash + the opposite of *dark*   _____

8. make + a word that rhymes with *retrieve*   _____

brand-new
upstairs
flashlight
make-believe
lifeguard
Thanksgiving
earthquake
seventy-five

Harcourt Brace School Publishers

Name _____

Before each sentence is a Spanish word that is commonly used in English. Contained in the sentence is a translation for the Spanish word. Decide what that translation is, and write it on the line.

1. *amigo:* My friend Pedro has two sisters.

   _____

2. *fiestas:* We have not had any celebrations since the spring planting.

   _____

3. *adobe:* Our home is built with sun-dried bricks made of clay and straw.

   _____

4. *mañana:* Tomorrow Miguel will keep watch.

   _____

5. *plaza:* In the middle of our fortress is a town square.

   _____

6. *gracias:* I said thank you to Don Hernando for allowing me to keep watch.

   _____

TRY THIS! Writing

Work with classmates to create a bulletin board display of words commonly used in English that come from other languages. Include words from Spanish, French, German, Japanese, and African languages.

Name _____

Read the following paragraphs and answer the questions that follow them.

The Southwestern Region features many kinds of landforms. This vast region includes rocky deserts, snow-capped mountains, and red mesas. There are also rainy plains, fertile river valleys, and deep canyons. People think of this land as being wild and untamed, and, in many parts, this is still true.

The states that make up the Southwestern Region are Arizona, New Mexico, Oklahoma, and Texas. Although there are only four states in this region, it is larger than the Northeast and the Great Lakes regions combined.

1. If you wrote a summary for these paragraphs, would you include the names of the states in the Southwestern Region? Why or why not?

   _____

   _____

2. Would you include a list of different landforms?

   _____

   _____

3. Write a summary of the paragraphs.

   _____

   _____

Harcourt Brace School Publishers

Name _____

Read the boldfaced words and definitions in the box below. Then choose a vocabulary word to complete each sentence in the job interview below.

piety:	reverence toward one's parents or religion
formal:	following set rules or patterns
compulsory:	required; necessary
room and board:	a place to live with meals provided
ingenious:	marked by special skill; clever

Mrs. Clarke

Mr. Summerfield

How many years of _____ education have you had, Mr. Summerfield?

I have been studying for twenty years, despite the fact that education is not _____ past the age of sixteen.

And would you say your degree of _____ is above average, Mr. Summerfield? We encourage loyalty and devotion here.

I try to live by the highest standards, Mrs. Clarke.

Your previous employer told me that your work was very creative and _____.

I always try to do my best in any job.

We cannot offer you a high salary, but we can offer you _____, which will keep your living expenses low.

I accept your offer, Mrs. Clarke. Thank you.

Write a description of your dream job. Include information about what kind of *formal* education would help you get it. Once you are hired, what tasks would be *compulsory* in order to be successful? In what *ingenious* ways would you do a better job than anyone else?

A. Summarize "Children of the Wild West" by completing the K-W-L chart.

K	W	L
What I Know	**What I Want to Know**	**What I Learned**

B. Explain to someone who has not read this selection what going to school in the Wild West was like.

_____

_____

_____

_____

Name _____

Read each statement below. Then look at the students in the picture. Use your imagination to write sentences about them. The first sentence has been done for you.

1. Compare the time when the teacher arrived at the school with the time when the students arrived. Use a form of the adverb *early*.

   On most days, the teacher arrived at school earlier than the students. _____

2. Compare how all the students in the school read. Use a form of the adverb *slowly*.

   _____

3. Compare the way Josh and Sarah solved math problems. Use a form of the adverb *easily*.

   _____

4. Compare the way Lena and Thomas wrote on their slates. Use a form of the adverb *neatly*.

   _____

5. Compare how all the students raced around the schoolhouse during recess. Use a form of the adverb *energetically*.

   _____

TRY THIS! Talking Tip

Tell a partner what you and other students at your school do during recess. Make at least one comparison using an adverb.

Name _____

A. You have been asked to help your school find teachers. Complete the
ads below by filling in the word that is related to the underlined word.

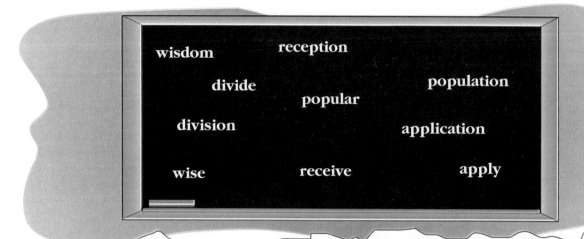

wisdom   reception

divide   population

popular

division   application

wise   receive   apply

1. Teacher Wanted!
   Make the <u>wise</u> choice. Share your
   _____
   with our children!

2. **GROWING POPULATION!**
   TEACHER PICKED BY
   _____ **VOTE.**

3. **TEACHERS:**
   <u>RECEIVE</u> FREE ROOM AND BOARD.
   A WARM _____
   AWAITS YOU.

4. TEACHER WANTED:
   NO NEED TO FILL OUT AN
   _____ .
   RIDE THE STAGECOACH TO OUR
   TOWN AND <u>APPLY</u> IN PERSON.
   THE JOB IS YOURS.

5. Can you read, write, and do long
   <u>division</u>? If so, you're the teacher for us.
   Come and _____ your
   time between teaching and panning for
   gold!

B. Complete each of the following pairs of related
words by filling in the missing letters. Then write
the words on the lines provided.

1. united   uni __ __   _____

2. athletic   athle __ __   _____

3. compete compet __ __ __ __ __   _____

athlete
unity
competitive
athletic
united
compete

Name _____

A. Read the following sentences from "Children of the Wild West." Look at the paraphrase of the first sentence. Then paraphrase the rest of the sentences.

Original Sentence	**Paraphrase**
1. The youngsters attended classes only as their chores and the weather allowed.	Children went to school only when they were able to.
2. Many youngsters were up at 4 A.M. milking cows, chopping wood, toting water, and helping fix breakfast before leaving for school.	_____ _____ _____
3. After a full day of classes, they might do other chores by moonlight so as not to miss the next day's classes.	_____ _____ _____

B. Read the following paragraph, and paraphrase it on the lines provided.

At one time only adult male property-owners could vote. In the 1800s, women began to speak out against this injustice. They became interested in politics, and they wanted to vote. States in the western part of the United States were the first to give women the vote. The Territory of Wyoming, for example, allowed women to vote as early as 1869. In 1890, Wyoming was granted statehood. It was the first state in which women could vote.

_____

_____

_____

_____

_____

_____

GO ON

Name _____

C. Read each sentence and its paraphrase. Then answer the questions.

1. Teachers were in great demand in the Wild West.

   Paraphrase: There was a shortage of teachers in the Wild West.

   Is this an accurate paraphrase? Explain your answer.

   _____

   _____

   _____

2. Teachers in the Wild West had a hard life because they received low pay and often had to live with the families of their students.

   Paraphrase: It was difficult for teachers to teach in the Wild West.

   Is this an accurate paraphrase? Explain your answer.

   _____

   _____

   _____

3. Education became required in California in 1874 for children between the ages of eight and fourteen.

   Paraphrase: Children did not always have to go to school.

   Is this an accurate paraphrase? Explain your answer.

   _____

   _____

   _____

In your Learning Log, write a paragraph about a trip you took or would like to take. Exchange your paragraph with a partner. Paraphrase each other's paragraphs.

Name _____

Read the following paragraphs. Then complete the outline below.

The smallest living parts of your body are cells. Although they are the building blocks of your body, you cannot see them unless you use a microscope. There are many different kinds of cells, such as bone cells and skin cells.

Tissues are groups of cells working together. Just as there are different kinds of cells, there are different kinds of tissues. Two kinds are fat tissue and muscle tissue. Each kind has a different function in your body.

When groups of tissues work together, organs are formed. Each organ does a different job; however, all of your organs need to work together for your body to operate successfully.

I. Cells

    A. _____

    B. _____

    C. _____

        1. _____

        2. _____

II. _____

    A. _____

    B. _____

        1. _____

        2. _____

    C. _____

III. _____

    A. _____

    B. _____

    C. _____

Harcourt Brace School Publishers

**Read the book reviews. Complete the exercise after each one.
Then complete the exercise at the end of both reviews.**

C. S. Lewis has done it again with his third book in the Chronicles of Narnia series—*The Horse and His Boy.* Those who are familiar with the first two books know that Narnia is a secret country known only to a few. In *The Horse and His Boy,* the reader meets a new hero and several new and unusual characters, including talking horses. This tale of a poor boy who is really a prince is sure to please current C. S. Lewis fans and new readers alike. Lewis is able to keep the reader's interest by including some familiar characters from the first two books and by introducing new ones.

1. Summarize the information you learned from this source.

_____

_____

_____

If you've read any of C. S. Lewis's books about the world between the lamppost and the castle—Narnia—you will want to pick up a copy of *Prince Caspian,* the fourth in the series. When Peter, Susan, Edmund, and Lucy are suddenly summoned back to Narnia, everyone wonders why. You'll find out! C. S. Lewis has created an exciting world where animals and people are equal and where good always triumphs over evil.

2. Summarize the information you learned from this source.

_____

_____

_____

3. Based on the book reviews you have read and the summaries you have written, write a conclusion that combines the information.

_____

_____

_____

_____

Name _____

**Read the boldfaced words and their definitions in the box . Then
complete the sentences that follow by writing the correct word
on the line provided.**

landscape:	natural scenery
bolster:	to support or prop up
entitled:	having a right to
baritone:	a male voice that is higher than a bass but lower than a tenor
able-bodied:	healthy and strong
pros and cons:	pluses and minuses; good points and bad points

1. Passengers on this train are _____ to an enjoyable ride.

2. If you get homesick, you can _____ your spirits by
   joining our singing group.

3. Our leader is a man who has a rich, deep, _____ voice.

4. Look through the window, and you'll see that the _____
   becomes more rugged here.

5. Once there was snow on the track, and all _____
   passengers had to get out and help clear it away.

6. In any discussion about the _____ of train travel,
   don't forget to mention that it's fun.

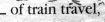

Writing

What does each vocabulary word make you think of? Do you think of mountains when you hear the word
landscape? Do you think of muscles when you hear the word *able-bodied*? For each vocabulary word,
make a list of related words. Exchange lists with a partner, and see whether your partner can match the
words on your list to the vocabulary words.

A. Complete the sequence chart about events in "A Family Apart."

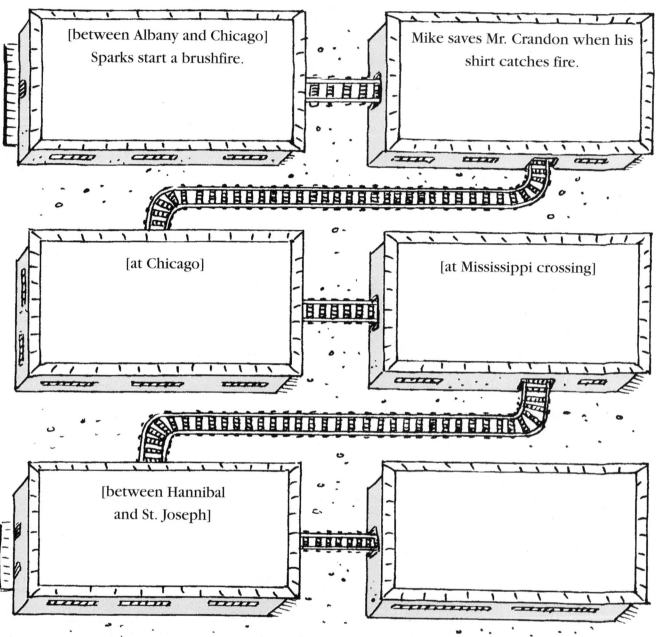

[between Albany and Chicago]
Sparks start a brushfire.

Mike saves Mr. Crandon when his
shirt catches fire.

[at Chicago]

[at Mississippi crossing]

[between Hannibal
and St. Joseph]

**B. What is the most important message about families that you learned
from this story?**

_____

_____

_____

_____

Name _____

Imagine that, like the children in "A Family Apart," you have traveled west on a train hoping to find a home with a new family. As you near the end of your trip, a reporter asks to interview you. Make up your own one-sentence answers to the reporter's questions. Include a negative in each answer.

Q: Which part of the trip was the most fun for you?

A: _____

Q: Which friends traveled west with you?

A: _____

Q: What frightened you the most during your trip?

A: _____

Q: What do you know about the new family you will live with?

A: _____

Q: What advice do you have for other children who might want to travel west to find new families?

A: _____

Q: What hopes do you have for your new life in the West?

A: _____

TRY THIS! Talking Tip

With a partner, take turns asking other interview questions. When it is your turn to answer, use a negative word in your sentence.

Harcourt Brace School Publishers

**A. Find and circle the eight misspelled words in the following paragraph.
Then write the correct spelling of each word on the line provided.**

half   island   palm   wreck   would   aisle   hymn   wrinkled

    Frances found her seat on the aile. She wondered whether her brothers and sisters woud ever be together again after the train ride. She hoped that at least haf the family would be placed in the same town. Frances hummed a hym silently to herself. It brought back memories of New York City, where they had lived. New York City was a crowded iland. Their new homes were likely to be in the middle of nowhere. How she dreaded the future! And if anyone found out she was a girl, that would reck everything. She became so nervous that the pam of her hand began to sweat. She rinkled her brow and worried about the future.

1. _____   4. _____   7. _____

2. _____   5. _____   8. _____

3. _____   6. _____

**B. Complete these words by filling in the missing silent letters. Then
write each word on the line provided.**

answer	wrap	gnaw	sword
reign	column	yolk	gnome

1. __ nome _____   5. rei __ n _____

2. ans __ er _____   6. colum __ _____

3. s __ ord _____   7. __ naw _____

4. yo __ k _____   8. __ rap _____

Harcourt Brace School Publishers

Name _____

A. Read the words in the box and the analogies below. Then complete each analogy by writing the correct word from the box in the space provided.

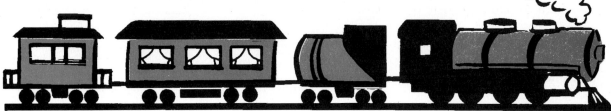

1. *Air* is to *airplane* as *water* is to _____.

2. *Soft* is to *silky* as *rough* is to _____.

3. *Chicago* is to *Illinois* as *St. Louis* is to _____.

4. *Steep* is to *level* as *crooked* is to _____.

5. *North* is to *south* as *east* is to _____.

6. *Yell* is to *loud* as _____ is to *quiet.*

7. _____ is to *ear* as *speak* is to *mouth.*

8. *Knee* is to *leg* as _____ is to *face.*

| Missouri |
| bumpy |
| steamboat |
| cheek |
| straight |
| west |
| whisper |
| listen |

B. Complete the following analogies with words of your own. Then explain the relationship between the words.

1. *Write* is to *paper* as *read* is to _____ .

2. *Exciting* is to *boring* as *awake* is to _____ .

3. *Flight attendant* is to *airplane* as *conductor* is to _____ .

4. *Avoid* is to *escape* as *try* is to _____ .

TRY THIS!
Writing

Work in small groups to create your own analogies. Leave out one word. Challenge other groups to fill in the missing word.

A. Read the following sentences. Tell which sense or senses each sentence appeals to—sight, hearing, smell, or touch.

1. The train rattled along the track, clickety-clack.   _____

2. The passengers looked frazzled and weather-beaten.   _____

3. The grass rustled as the wind swept across the plains.   _____

4. The smooth, silky dress glimmered under the moonlight.   _____

5. The sweet fragrance of the bright red flowers filled the air.   _____

B. Read the topics below. For each topic, make a web with images and sensory words to describe the topic.

Topic One: Summer

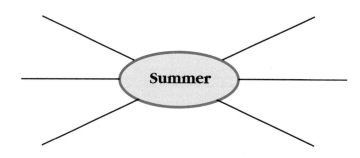

Topic Two: Waves

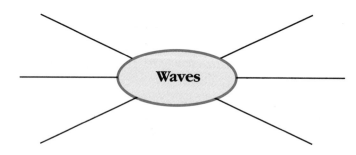

Name _____

Topic Three: Music

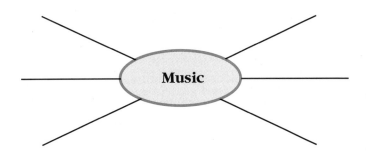

Topic Four: School

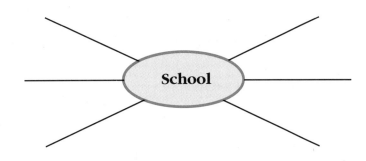

C. Select one of the topics for which you made a web. Write a paragraph about this topic in which you use imagery and sensory words.

_____

_____

_____

_____

_____

_____

In your Learning Log, write down the names of the five senses. For each one, write a word that would appeal to that particular sense—for example: SIGHT—bright; TOUCH—coarse.

**Read the following paragraphs. Then paraphrase each
paragraph. The first one has been done for you.**

The first railroad in the United States was built in 1830. New York and
Chicago were connected in 1853, but it wasn't until 1856 that railroad tracks
went west of the Mississippi.

Early trains were pulled by steam engines. Wood was burned in the engine of
the train to produce steam. These engines also produced a great amount of smoke
and a lot of noise.

The railroad became a popular means of travel as pioneer families moved
west. The trips were long and tedious, but they could also be exciting. Trains
were sometimes robbed by outlaws. Once in a while, sparks from the train
would ignite a brushfire.

1. Paraphrase the first paragraph.

The railroad system in the United States grew slowly over many years. _____

2. Paraphrase the second paragraph.

_____

_____

_____

3. Paraphrase the third paragraph.

_____

_____

_____

4. Write a short summary of the three paragraphs.

_____

_____

_____

Name _____

The front of each of these trading cards has a vocabulary word and a definition. The back of each has a list of related words. Which front goes with which back? Draw lines to match each vocabulary word with its related words.

citizens:
people born in or made members of a country

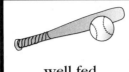

well fed
comfortable home
savings account

spokesperson:
someone who speaks on behalf of a group

borders
passports
visas

home
apartment
suburb

residential:
suitable for homes

vote
pay taxes
make an oath of allegiance

immigrant:
a person who comes into a new country to make a new home

prosperous:
successful, flourishing, thriving

great-grandmother
family tree
generations

ancestors:
persons from whom one is descended, usually persons who lived before one's grandparents

representative
speaker
communicator

TRY THIS!
Writing

On a separate piece of paper, write a story about your family, using as many of the vocabulary words and related words as you can.

**A. Summarize "Hector Lives in the United States Now" by completing
the K-W-L chart.**

K	W	L
What I Know	**What I Want to Know**	**What I Learned**

B. What message did you learn from this story?

_____

_____

_____

_____

_____

Name _____

A. Rosalia wrote this letter during her summer vacation. As you read the letter, find and underline the ten prepositional phrases.

Dear Celia,

My sister and I arrived in Mexico City last Friday. We are staying with my grandparents right now. They have a big house near the center of the city. Later, we will stay with my aunt and uncle. Their house is near the beach—that should be fun! I like being here with my relatives, but I miss you and my other friends in Chicago. I'll see you at the end of the month.

Your best friend,
Rosalia

B. Celia wrote back to her friend Rosalia, but she didn't include enough details to make her letter interesting. Rewrite this paragraph from Celia's letter. Add at least one prepositional phrase to each sentence.

So far, my vacation has been pretty boring. I hope you will come back soon. My parents and I will be traveling. Maybe you can come.

_____

_____

_____

_____

Choose one object in the classroom. Don't name the object, but give your partner hints about it. For each hint, complete this sentence with a prepositional phrase: *It's _____.* See how many hints you have to give before your partner guesses the object.

Harcourt Brace School Publishers

A. Hector's class is studying the countries of the world and their peoples. Correct the underlined words in this report. Write the correct spelling of each word on the line provided.

Before Hector came to the United States, he lived in a country called <u>Mexeco</u>. Hector's family speaks Spanish, and their ancestors are <u>Mexicun</u>. He was not born in the United States, but his brothers were. They are <u>Amerrican</u> citizens. Hector and his family live in a neighborhood with people from countries in Central and South <u>america</u>.

One country Hector is studying is in Southeast Asia, where a lot of fighting has taken place. This country is called <u>Vietnom</u>, and almost all of its 62 million people are <u>Vietnamise</u>. It is about the size of New Mexico. Most people there are farmers.

There is a country in Europe that has castles, a clock named Big Ben, and double-decker buses. It is called <u>Englend</u>. The United States was once a colony of this country. People who live there speak <u>english</u>, just as they do in the United States. Another country in Europe hosted the first Olympic Games—<u>Grece</u>. This country consists of small peninsulas, and it is where one early civilization flourished. This <u>Greec</u> civilization was responsible for creating a democratic form of government.

1. _____ 6. _____

2. _____ 7. _____

3. _____ 8. _____

4. _____ 9. _____

5. _____ 10. _____

American	England
America	Vietnamese
English	Greek
Mexico	Greece
Mexican	Vietnam

B. Complete the sentences with words from the box. Write each word on the line provided.

1. This is a continent where you can go on a safari and see many animals like lions and elephants. This continent is _____. A person who lives on this continent is called an _____.

2. This country is famous for producing cars and electronic equipment. Its most famous city is Tokyo. This country is _____. Almost everyone in this country speaks _____.

3. The continent where Japan, Korea, and China are located is called _____.

   A general name given to a person who lives on this continent is _____.

Japan
Japanese
Asia
Asian
Africa
African

Harcourt Brace School Publishers

Name _____

A. Read each of the following sentences. Then underline the word in parentheses that has the more positive connotation.

1. Hector's family has always been (thrifty, stingy) about spending money on luxuries.

2. Hector's (group, gang) of friends likes to play baseball.

3. One day the baseball field was (drenched, soggy).

4. Some other children are always (spying on, observing) Hector and his friends.

5. After Hector hits a home run, he (smiles, smirks) at the pitcher.

6. Hector's mother enjoys (gossiping, chatting) with her neighbors.

7. Hector tries not to (gripe, complain) about school too much.

8. Hector's father wants his sons to be (ambitious, pushy).

Harcourt Brace School Publishers

Name _____

B. Read what each character is saying. Determine whether the words have a positive or negative connotation. Then rewrite each statement so that it has the opposite connotation.

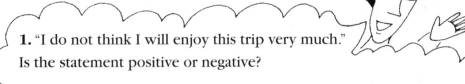

1. "I do not think I will enjoy this trip very much."
Is the statement positive or negative?

_____

_____

2. "This should be an amazing adventure!"
Is the statement positive or negative?

_____

_____

3. "I don't know why I even bothered to pack."
Is the statement positive or negative?

_____

_____

4. "We will probably have a great time!"
Is the statement positive or negative?

_____

_____

TRY THIS!
Writing

Look for examples of words with positive or negative connotations in editorials or letters to the editor found in newspapers. List some of these. Next to each word, write a synonym that has a different connotation. Share your list.

Name _____

A. Read the following test questions. As you answer them, think about the strategies you could use.

Fill in the circle in front of the word or phrase that correctly completes each sentence.

1. The United States is bordered on the north by _____.

   ○ Mexico   ○ Bermuda

   ○ Canada   ○ Iceland

2. The ocean that forms the eastern boundary of the United States is the _____.

   ○ Indian Ocean   ○ Atlantic Ocean

   ○ Pacific Ocean   ○ Arctic Ocean

3. The capital of the United States is _____.

   ○ New York City   ○ Philadelphia

   ○ Seattle, Washington   ○ Washington, D.C.

4. The longest river in the United States is the _____.

   ○ Hudson River   ○ Missouri River

   ○ Mississippi River   ○ Colorado River

5. The United States is bordered on the south by _____.

   ○ Mexico   ○ New Mexico

   ○ Canada   ○ Iceland

6. The last two states to become part of the United States were _____.

   ○ Hawaii and Idaho   ○ Alaska and Idaho

   ○ Hawaii and Alaska   ○ Alaska and Montana

GO ON ▷

Name _____

B. Answer the following questions about test-taking strategies.

1. What should you do when you get a test paper?

   _____

   _____

2. Look at question 2. How would you go about identifying the answer?

   _____

   _____

   _____

   _____

3. Look at question 5. What would you do if you knew the countries to the north but not to the south of the United States?

   _____

   _____

   _____

   _____

4. What should you do if you don't know the answer to a question?

   _____

   _____

5. Once you've completed the test, what should you do?

   _____

   _____

Work with a partner. In your Learning Log, write a booklet of test-taking tips to share with younger students.

Harcourt Brace School Publishers

Name _____

Read the following paragraphs. Then complete the activities that follow.

The Statue of Liberty, a gift from the French people to the American people, has stood in New York Harbor since 1886. It was designed by French sculptor Frédéric-Auguste Bartholdi and was originally called *Liberty Enlightening the World.* In 1986, for its centennial celebration, the statue was restored and given a new torch. Every year millions of people visit this symbol of welcome to all.

Ellis Island, located near the Statue of Liberty in New Jersey waters, is part of the Statue of Liberty National Monument. It has its own museum, which opened in 1990. The Ellis Island Immigration Museum honors all the immigrants who entered the United States from 1892 to 1932 looking for a new beginning.

1. Paraphrase the first paragraph.

_____

_____

_____

_____

_____

_____

GO ON

2. Write a summary statement about the first paragraph.

_____

_____

_____

_____

3. Paraphrase the second paragraph.

_____

_____

_____

_____

_____

4. Write a summary statement about the second paragraph.

_____

_____

_____

_____

5. Write a summary statement about the whole article.

_____

_____

_____

_____

_____

_____

Harcourt Brace School Publishers

SKILLS AND STRATEGIES INDEX

VOCABULARY

Abbreviations 151

Acronyms 151

Analogies 175

Antonyms 14

Aviation Words 85

Connotation/Denotation 29, 183, 184

Drama Terms 69

Foreign Words 135, 159

Homographs 44

Homophones 36

Key Words 3, 10, 18, 25, 32, 40, 49, 57, 65, 73, 81, 89, 95, 102, 108, 117, 125, 131, 139, 147, 155, 163, 171, 179

Music Words 121

Specialized Vocabularies 112

Synonyms 7

COMPREHENSION

Compare and Contrast 93, 94, 101, 115

Context Clues/ Multiple-Meaning Words 99, 100, 107, 124

Fact and Opinion/ Author's Purpose/ Author's Viewpoint 37, 38, 47, 48, 56

Main Idea and Details 129, 130, 138, 145

Make Generalizations 15, 16, 23

Make Predictions/Draw Conclusions 30, 39, 55

Making Judgments 22, 31

Narrative Elements

characters, settings, plot, theme 70, 71, 80, 86

point of view 106, 116

Paraphrase 167, 168

Sequence/Cause and Effect 8, 9, 17, 24

Summarize 160, 161

Summarize/Paraphrase 178, 187, 188

Summarize the Literature 4, 11, 19, 26, 33, 41, 50, 58, 66, 74, 82, 90, 96, 103, 109, 118, 126, 132, 140, 148, 156, 164, 172, 180

Synthesize Information 143, 144, 170

LITERARY APPRECIATION

Imagery 176, 177

Literary Devices:

Figurative Language 45, 46, 64

Slanted/Biased Writing 122, 123

DECODING

Structural Analysis 136, 137, 146, 154

SPELLING

brought, full 35

Compound Words 158

-ed, -ing 60, 68

Long Vowels 13, 21

noise, town 28

Places and People 182

Prefixes

dis-, de- 120

pre-, pro- 105

un-, re-, in-, inter- 111

Related Words 166

/s/, /z/, /sh/ 52

Short Vowels 6

"Silent" Letters 174

Suffixes

-ible, -able 92

-ion 98

Unstressed Endings

/ən/ and /ər/ 76

/əl/ 84

VCCV 128

VCCCV 134

VCV 142

VV 150

Vowels Before *r* 43

Harcourt Brace School Publishers

SKILLS AND STRATEGIES INDEX

Harcourt Brace School Publishers